About the A

Hayley and Bill are lifelong , and photograph recipes for their popular website, rimal-palate.com. Their site has become one of the most trusted Paleo recipe websites on the internet, and their loyal following continues to grow. A genuine love of food and health, combined with a uniquely artistic eye for styling and photography, are signature characteristics of their work.

Hayley and Bill's first cookbook, *Make it Paleo*, continues to be a national bestseller, and boasts over 200 delicious recipes. It takes the reader on a culinary journey that offers something for everyone, from the basics to family favorites to exotic cuisines from around the world—all improved upon and made Paleo. It is a must-have cookbook in any grain-free kitchen.

After the release of *Make it Paleo*, Hayley and Bill refocused their creative talents on improving their website, with interactive features like recipe filters, a meal planner, a smart phone app (called "myKitchen"), and the ability for users to upload their own recipes—all of which are free. After months of site improvements, the pair longed to get back in the kitchen to do what they do best—cook! The result: Their second cookbook, *Gather—The Art of Paleo Entertaining*, and now *The 30 Day Guide to Paleo Cooking*.

When they're not in the kitchen cooking, they enjoy working out in their basement gym, gardening together, and traveling to new places. They live in Pittsburgh with their new puppy, Charlie, and their two cats, Lexi and Belly (all three were rescued), and are planning their August 2013 wedding!

Contents

the 30 Day Guide to Paleo Cooking

by Hayley Mason and Bill Staley
bestselling authors of *Make it Paleo* and *Gather*

Victory Belt Publishing Inc.
Las Vegas

First Published in 2013 by Victory Belt Publishing

ISBN: 978-1-936608-49-2
Printed in The USA
RRD 01-13

Book design, layout, and photography by Bill Staley and Hayley Mason.
Additional photo credits:
Pg 9 - Chea "after photo" by Miki Vargas Photography
Pg 14 - Pig photo by Heather Lahtinen
Pg 31 - Junk food cupboard photo by Leslie Hester
Pg 37 - Fruit and vegetable plate photo
        (and *Make it Paleo* cover photo) by Kelli Beavers

For more recipe inspiration, visit www.PrimalPalate.com
Also by Hayley and Bill:
   Make it Paleo (2011)
   Gather—The Art of Paleo Entertaining (2013)

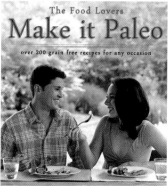

Paleo Success Stories

My before photo is from three years ago, when I first started changing my lifestyle. I had been following the bodybuilder's diet to a "T": lean meats, "good" carbs, limited fats, and no sugar. Like many bodybuilders, I ate "fat-free" and "sugar-free" artificial "food" because I thought it was good for me. You would think that with no sugar or fat in my diet, I would have lost a lot of body fat, but because I was stuffing myself with protein and whole grains every 2 to 3 hours, I was constantly bloated and uncomfortable. I also relied on caffeine to get the energy I needed throughout the day and pre-workout. Eventually I became concerned that my body was reacting negatively to something I was eating. Shortly after, a friend told me about the Paleo diet; she explained that grains are toxic to our bodies. I decided to give Paleo a try for 30 days to see if I was gluten intolerant. Sure enough, within that time, my stomach flattened, I lost more weight than I had in months, I had more energy than I knew what to do with, and I felt amazing! It took just 30 days for me to see and feel serious results, but it has taken me years to transform my body and mind. Going Paleo has completely changed me, inside and out.

I am now the leanest I have ever been. I sleep deeply, I have a huge amount of natural energy, my skin is clearer, and I feel amazing. Bill and Hayley's recipes—on their site and in their cookbook, *Make It Paleo*—have been a big part of my transformation. I absolutely love this lifestyle and I want everyone to experience the changes I have!

Name: Chrissy B.
Age: 24
Time to Reach Goal: 3 years
Best Paleo Benefit: Consistent, natural energy.
Favorite Paleo Dish: Baked chicken thighs

• •

I started following a Paleo lifestyle in November 2011. At the age of 40, I was on two different blood pressure medications, I had asthma and, despite taking Prilosec twice a day, I suffered greatly from acid reflux. I was depressed, exhausted, and had an awful case of Candida which sent me looking for natural, alternative medical options. My new naturopath told me to change my eating habits and gave me a long list of stuff to avoid, but no information about what I could eat. I was never a fan of vegetables and struggled for a month to feed myself. I wandered the grocery store aisles aimlessly and would leave hungry and in tears. Then, one day, I stumbled upon some Paleo recipes online and my life changed forever!

Within three months of going Paleo, I was off all of my prescription medications and had lost nearly 40 pounds! My health is so much better; I no longer have any asthma issues or acid reflux—even when eating trigger foods like onions and garlic. My blood pressure is within normal ranges and I have way more energy. I will never eat processed, sugary foods again!

Name: Leah B.
Age: 40
Time to Reach Goal: 12 months
Best Paleo Benefit: Feeling good and getting off medication.
Favorite Paleo Dish: If I had to pick just one, it would be the Roasted Rosemary Beets. I never would have eaten beets before!

Name: Jeanne S.
Age: 47
Time to Reach Goal: 18 months
Best Paleo Benefit: Improved health. I am no longer pre-diabetic and that is priceless!
Favorite Paleo Dish: Fennel and orange salad—delicious!

Eighteen months ago I was 130 pounds overweight, weighing 265 pounds. I was suffering from metabolic syndrome, pre-diabetes, sleep apnea, high blood pressure, high cholesterol, depression, chronic fatigue syndrome, adrenal fatigue, and hypothyroidism. I decided it was time to take control of the situation. I began working out with my son, who is a personal trainer. After my first session, I decided there was no way I was going to work that hard and then go home and ruin it with bad food. The first thing I did was eliminate sugar from my diet. As I began to see results, I became inspired and decided to follow a Paleo diet, which is something my son had been trying to get me to do for awhile. The weight started dropping off quickly after that. My son bought me the *Make it Paleo* cookbook for my birthday. It remains my favorite Paleo cookbook. I have now lost about 110 pounds and am working to lose a little more. I have never felt better. I have gone from taking 14 medications to just my thyroid pill. The Paleo diet has basically saved my life.

• •

Name: Doug P.
Age: 35
Time to Reach Goal: 6 months
Best Paleo Benefit: Increased energy throughout the day, with almost no fluctuations in the blood sugar levels that lead to cravings and unhealthy snacking.
Favorite Paleo Dish: Almond-crusted fried chicken.

As a U.S. Marine, I had been "in shape"—or at least what I considered to be in shape. I was always exercising, but I never felt like I was fit or healthy. In 2010, I came off of active duty service, and within a year of that transition my life spiraled out of control. Fat, borderline alcoholic, and wolfing down every Twinkie and pizza in sight, I quickly gained 40 pounds. At 5'7" and 220 pounds, I was considered obese. I worked long hours at a high-stress corporate job that I hated, and I missed living an active lifestyle. Eating was how I dealt with my depression. In 2011, at the age of 57, my mother died suddenly of a heart attack. That was when I realized that unless I was willing to take control of my health, I was heading in the same direction. Right then and there I decided that I would not let my health go down the drain. I joined a local CrossFit gym because it fit perfectly with my "no time to exercise" corporate schedule, and that's where I first heard members discussing the Paleo diet. When the gym posted a 30-day Paleo challenge, I decided to give it a shot. I've never looked back. Not only did I drop all the extra weight within a year, I am at my fittest and healthiest ever. The one-two punch of CrossFit and a Paleo diet has completely changed my life. I now dedicate my time to spreading the word about healthy, clean eating. I've quit the corporate gig to become a CrossFit coach and personal trainer in San Diego.

I'm 5'6", 23 years old, and have always been active. However, up until May 2010 I had never paid attention to my nutrition; I ate whatever I wanted, whenever I wanted, with no regard to the nutritional value of the food. I was 180 pounds and a size 12 or 14 when I decided to get serious about taking care of my body. I started my journey with P90X, and moved on to Insanity and Insanity Asylum. I also trained for and ran a half marathon in November 2010.

By the beginning of 2011, I had lost 30 pounds and was down to a size 8. I was eating the Standard American Diet (SAD), but I was counting calories. I didn't realize it at the time, but I was constantly tired and thinking about the next meal. I stumbled across CrossFit and the Paleo lifestyle in January of 2011. Intrigued, I did further research and decided to give them both a shot. Immediately, my energy levels shot up, my eczema went away, and my overall mood improved immensely. I also lost an additional 20 pounds. I was finally putting the right foods into my body, as opposed to processed wheat products with minimal nutritional value—the kind of food that would just tide me over until my next meal. I learned about the value of macro- and micro-nutrients and how they play into every aspect of our physiological functions. I'm proud to say that I still follow a Paleo lifestyle and am an avid CrossFitter. I believe that advocating the Paleo lifestyle is a great step towards educating the world on the importance of natural, whole foods.

· ·

I've been eating Paleo since July 2011, and it has changed my life more than I ever imagined possible. I found the diet because I was tired of being fat—my beginning weight was a little more than 340 pounds—and dealing with all the issues that come with that. I started to feel better within the first few weeks of eating Paleo. Now, nearly two years later, I'm a completely different person. I have better energy, feel healthier, and have gotten rid of the health problems caused by the "normal" American diet. I currently weight around 200 pounds (I say around because I don't use a scale) and live a happy, active life: I am more positive and rise to meet all the challenges life throws at me. I truly believe that changing to a Paleo lifestyle has saved my life.

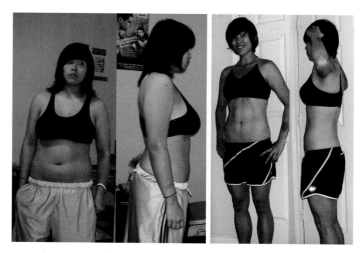

Name: Grace L.
Age: 23
Time to Reach Goal: 1 year
Best Paleo Benefit: Increased knowledge of the value of whole foods and fueling your body the right way.
Favorite Paleo Dish: I like pretty much any Paleo dish, but you can never go wrong with the classic breakfast: 2 eggs over easy (or poached), bacon, and sweet potato hash. I love dipping the bacon and sweet potato in the gooey egg yolk.

Name: Steve G.
Age: 31
Time to Reach Goal: Lost 50 pounds in 7 weeks; 140 pounds in 10 months
Best Paleo Benefit: Stress reduction. When it comes to food, I focus on quality not quantity; by not counting every calorie I eat, my life is simpler and happier. Instead I eat what I need in the amounts that I need and leave it at that.
Favorite Paleo Dish: Chili. It's hard to pick one because you can do it so many ways. I love spicy things and you can really bring some heat to chili.

Name: Jamison C.
Age: 29
Time to Reach Goal: Lost over 100 pounds in 7 months
Best Paleo Benefit: Waking up knowing that I am in the best shape of my life... and it only gets better every day.
Favorite Paleo Dish: London broil or Bill and Hayley's carrot cake. (Damn, that cake is good!)

On the morning of June 4th 2010, I found myself lying in the cardiac ward of my local hospital, surrounded by doctors and nurses. I was just 26 years old. It was a wake up call—my body was screaming that it was time to make a change and adopt a healthier lifestyle.

Since then I've taken deliberate steps to gain control of my health. With the tough love of my best friend Mark, many miles put on my internal odometer, tons of burpees, and the switch to a Paleo lifestyle, I'm proud to say I've lost 100 pounds and dropped from a 44 inch waist to a 34.

Bill and Hayley have literally saved my life. I'm proof that even a bachelor can cook their simple, quick, easy-to-follow recipes. Even better, when I cook for non-Paleo friends, they demand the recipes because everything tastes so great. I gladly point them to Bill and Hayley's website, www.primalpalate.com.

. . . .

Name: Chae F.
Age: 28
Time to Reach Goal: The initial goal was to complete the 30-day challenge—3 months to lose 30 pounds.
Best Paleo Benefit: Having a connection to real food again!
Favorite Paleo Dish: Coconut curry seafood stew served over cauliflower rice.

I've made many mistakes on my journey to better health, and I've learned more about myself than I ever could have imagined, both good and bad. I went from a top weight of 300 pounds in 2006 to 190 pounds in 2009, and then could not lose a pound more. I started working with a trainer and was so inspired by him that I decided do the same for others: I got certified. But I quickly learned that even though I knew a lot about kicking butt, I didn't know much about proper nutrition. I was still living under the grand illusion that whole wheat bread, pasta, and high fiber cereal were healthy and good for me. Then I heard about the Paleo lifestyle. I bought Robb Wolf's book, *The Paleo Solution*, and, not even halfway through it, decided to try the 30-day challenge. That was 10 months ago. I haven't looked back since. Not only have I managed to drop another 30 pounds, I was able to reverse the devastating effects of alopecia areata (I was balding at 20) and severe eczema and psoriasis (which painful steroid treatments and topical ointments prescribed by doctors had done nothing for). Not only that, I have the energy of kid: I feel unstoppable. More importantly, I discovered how to love myself. Living clean has given me the gift of a life that I knew I wanted but didn't believe I deserved. Now I dedicate my life to showing others that they, too, deserve a good life—a life they can have as soon as they love themselves enough to change.

Introduction

Give yourself a pat on the back. By picking up *The 30 Day Guide to Paleo Cooking*, you are consciously making a decision to eat better. In this book, we will guide you through your first month of the Paleo diet. We explain everything that you need to know, beginning with a basic understanding of why this way of eating promotes optimal health and vitality. We are all designed to be fit, healthy, happy people—it's in our genes! The Paleo diet allows our genes to express their natural tendency towards vibrant health.

For many people, making big dietary changes—let alone going on a "diet"—is overwhelming, even scary. Don't worry, this is not a diet book—not even close. We are using the word diet in the most traditional sense, as in the nutrition your body needs. We focus on the first 30 days of a Paleo diet because that's when you'll need our guidance the most. But make no mistake: This is a guide to eating healthier for the rest of your life. We have helped thousands of people take the Paleo plunge.

Set aside any reservations you may have about adopting this lifestyle. We're going to make it easy and fun, as well as incredibly tasty! At the core, what we do, even beyond this book, is

provide the healthiest and most delicious recipes within a Paleo framework.

We start off by tackling the Paleo diet basics: What to eat and what to avoid. We briefly touch on the many health benefits, and you've read the testimonials from some of our greatest success stories.

You'll learn about the major food groups in the Paleo diet, and how to best select ingredients. By far the biggest stumbling block for beginners is uncertainty over what is or isn't a Paleo food. You will have no confusion after reading Part 1, where we clearly identify the food groups. After that, we'll detail how to build a meal and how to make a Paleo-friendly shopping list.

Friends, family, and co-workers will no doubt have a lot of questions about your new diet—particularly regarding gluten, fat, cholesterol,

calcium, and carbohydrates. We promise that once you're done reading this book, you'll be equipped to answer them.

Your 30 day meal plan begins in Part 2. It's simple and adaptable enough that everyone can be successful. You get recipes for every meal of every day for a month. In our hectic world, it's unreasonable to think that you will have the time to cook three meals every day. This is why we include several larger meals each week, which will provide you with leftovers for a following day. (The meal plans and the accompanying shopping lists are reprinted as tear-outs in the back of the book; you can also find them on our website.)

Part 3 is where you'll find the recipes—most of which are referenced in the meal plan. These are some of our tastiest, easiest, and "cleanest" dishes. You won't be finding recipes in this book

for "Paleo brownies" or treats. Your first 30 days of eating Paleo are about eliminating the junky, processed foods you've been attached to for years—perhaps your whole life! We'll show you how to strip down to the cleanest and healthiest choices. If you want to reward yourself after your first 30 days, visit our website www.primalpalate.com and browse through dozens of decadent treats. Until then, no peeking!

We feel confident that at the end of your first 30 days you're going feel better than ever. Give the Paleo diet an honest shot and you will see results. For some people that means the possibility of alleviating chronic pain or inflammation. For others it means potential weight loss. For most people it means feeling greatly improved vitality and health. Good luck, and happy cooking!

- Hayley and Bill

Part 1: What is the Paleo Diet?

The Paleo diet is based upon eating the foods our bodies were designed for through thousands of years of evolution. These foods were available to early people through hunting and gathering: meat and fish, nuts and seeds, fruits and vegetables. With advances in technology, other kinds of food became available for consumption—grains, dairy, and processed foods—which are not as easy for our bodies to digest. The foods recommended in the Paleo diet generally provide our bodies with more efficient, long-lasting energy that also aids in burning fat.

We Say Paleo... You Say Primal

"Primal" generally refers to Mark Sisson's *The Primal Blueprint*; it is essentially the Paleo diet with fewer dairy and saturated fat restrictions. Throughout this book, the terms "Paleo" and "Primal" are used interchangeably, and many people who follow this way of eating consider them to be one and the same. Generally speaking, Paleo refers to a high protein, moderate fat diet, and Primal to a high fat, moderate protein diet. You are free to call this meal plan what you want because, bottom line, both diets stem from the core principle of eating the foods that our bodies were designed to eat: plants and animals.

Enjoy

Meats

Vegetables

Fruits

Nuts

Seeds

Healthy Fats

Avoid

Grains

Legumes

Processed Dairy

Processed Foods

Alcohol

Soy

Intuitive Eating

The Paleo diet is not "one size fits all." Sure, these guidelines provide a set of rules that you can easily remember. But in our minds the Paleo diet is more about intuitive eating. In other words, you should be actively thinking about what you put in your mouth. To start, read any and all food labels. Are there ingredients in that jar of mustard that are not natural? If so, then it isn't your best choice.

Beyond the lists of do's and don'ts, it is occasionally acceptable to eat full-fat and raw dairy, starchy vegetables, and natural sugars. However, if you are looking to achieve the maximum health benefits of a Paleo diet, sticking strictly to whole foods and minimal treats will provide the best avenue to success.

Hayley Mason and Bill Staley

Protein: Meat, Fish and Fowl

As part of a grain-free lifestyle, you will need to invest in quality food. That means making sure that any meat or dairy products you purchase come from animals that were fed the diet they were meant to consume. It also means choosing wild-caught fish and avoiding varieties that are threatened or endangered. Eating animals or fish that were raised in appropriate conditions not only contributes to your health, it supports the health of our planet.

"Red" Meat

As we mentioned, whenever possible, choose grass-fed, pasture-raised organic meat. If grain-fed is your only option, look for leaner cuts to avoid consuming the toxins stored in the fat of grain-fed animals.

- Beef
- Lamb
- Bison
- Venison
- Goat

As a rule of thumb, look to buy organic, grass-fed meats, wild-caught fish, and pasture-raised poultry. If possible, it is also best to purchase your meat directly from a farmer. This way you will not only be supporting local farming, you will be sure of the quality of the product you are buying. Part of making good food choices is researching and thinking about what you are buying.

Pork

Pork can be a little tricky. Pigs are like living, breathing disposal units; they can and will eat anything and everything. So when it comes to pork, make sure that you are purchasing meat from pigs that were lovingly raised on a farm and fed a non-GMO (genetically modified) diet.

Poultry

When choosing poultry, pasture-raised is best. This means you are consuming animals that were allowed to roam freely, feeding on bugs and other insects rather than grain. If there are no local farms selling chickens, then organic, free-range chickens from a store are the next best thing. A free-range chicken is happier and healthier, which will make you healthier and happier.

- Chicken
- Turkey
- Duck
- Pheasant
- Goose

Seafood

Go for wild-caught seafood whenever possible. Fish is your best option for obtaining a good amount of omega-3 fatty acids from food, which is always preferable to supplements. In addition, try to buy fish caught using sustainable and ethical fishing practices. Our top ten seafood options to enjoy:

- Alaskan Salmon
- Yellowfin Tuna
- Mahi-Mahi
- Shrimp
- Sardines
- Snapper
- Mussels
- Crab
- Lobster
- Cod

Eggs

If you can't find a local source of pastured eggs, your best option is to enjoy the organic, omega-3-enriched variety. Pastured eggs come from chickens that feed freely on bugs, grass, and vegetable scraps. Omega-3-enriched eggs come from chickens that are fed a diet of flax-supplemented corn and soy (the flax increases the omega-3 content).

Fruits and Vegetables

You will find a large array of fruits and vegetables in this book. We are big fans of growing our own produce, or getting it from local farmers and farmers' markets whenever possible—which, in many parts of the northern hemisphere means late April through October. Another way of receiving fresh produce is by participating in a CSA (Community Supported Agriculture) program. Through a CSA, a farmer sends his or her best crops to a specified drop point near you. This is a great way to support local family farms.

If you have a green thumb and a sunny spot, you can try your hand at growing your own herbs and vegetables. Even if you do not have a yard, it is relatively simple to grow some basic herbs in a small planter on a sunny windowsill. If you have a yard, even better! We like to grow lettuce, beets, broccoli, peppers, and a whole slew of herbs (lemon thyme, rosemary, basil, oregano and chives, to name a few). There is no better salad than one with fresh veggies from your garden! To complete the circle of sustainable gardening, we compost plant-based, soil-enriching table scraps.

But what if you do not have time to tend to a garden, and there are no farmers markets nearby? That's okay, because there are often plenty of options in your local grocery store. When shopping for fruits and vegetables, it is often better to buy 'organic' items, because they will have the least amount of chemicals and pesticides involved in their production.

Certain crops tend to absorb pesticides more than others. You should only buy these fruits and vegetables if they are organic:

- strawberries
- spinach
- bell peppers
- nectarines
- lettuce
- pears
- apples
- celery
- peaches
- cherries
- grapes
- potatoes

As a final note, we recommend buying your produce in season. It will be cheaper, easier to find, and the incredible taste of freshly picked vegetables and fruit can't be beat.

Seasonal produce varies from region to region in North America and Europe. The list of fruits and vegetables on the next page is meant to show what is generally available during different times of year. Many of these varieties are in grocery stores year-round, but the freshest and most sustainable sources are always seasonal and local. When possible, support local farmers through CSA programs, farmers' markets, and buying directly from farm stands. Even then, look for the farmers who grow crops using organic practices.

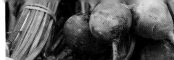

Summer

apples
avocado
basil
bell peppers
berries
carrots
cherries
cilantro
cucumbers
eggplant
figs
garlic
green beans
mangoes
melons
nectarines
okra
peaches
peppers
summer squash
tomatoes
zucchini

Spring

apricots
artichokes
asparagus
grapefruit
green onions
leeks
lemons
lettuce
mint
mushrooms
parsley
radishes
rhubarb
spinach
spring onions
strawberries
wild greens

Winter

beets
belgian endive
cabbage
celery
citrus
clementines
escarole
horseradish
kiwi
mandarins
onions
parsnips
pears
pomelos
rutabagas
sweet potatoes
turnips

Fall

arugula
broccoli
brussels sprouts
cauliflower
collards
chiles
cranberries
curly endive
fennel
grapes
kale
lemongrass
limes
pomegranates
pumpkin
shallots
swiss chard
winter squash

Growing Your Own Food

Few things are as rewarding as being able to grow your own food! Don't be deterred if you think you have a brown thumb. All you need for a vibrant garden is a spot with 6 or more hours of direct sun, good soil, and regular watering. Yes, there's a little more to it than that, but the basics are easily tackled by just about anyone. Here's what you need to make your garden grow.

Water

It probably won't come as news to you that water is the most critical element for growing plants. Anyone who has sprouted garlic in a glass of water can tell you that. But how much, exactly? Too little water and the plant will dry out and die; too much and you will drown it. If growing from a container garden, you will need to keep a close eye on how much water you are providing. Although the soil does not need to be damp at all times, generally you will want to water most plants every day when it is hot and sunny, and every other day when temperatures are cooler. Of course, if you are getting adequate natural rainfall, you won't need to supplement at all.

Sunlight

A close second to water is sunlight. Plants derive their energy from the sun through a process called photosynthesis—something we all learned about in school when we were kids. (Animals depend on photosynthesis for energy too, which is why we can't survive without plant life.) Therefore, a good spot for a vegetable garden receives an abundance of direct sunlight. If your garden is getting 6 or more hours of sun in a day, that is considered adequate for growing. But what will really make your garden grow during the summer? Eight hours or more!

Soil

Good soil is the third critical element. Most people have poor soil in their yards, meaning that it is too sandy or rocky or made entirely of clay. You will probably need to help the dirt along by adding organic matter. In addition, garden soil has to drain adequately, retaining just the right amount of water (too much is not good). There are numerous websites devoted to organic gardening, including seedsofchange.com and organicgardeing.com. Or you can also check to see if there is a local garden store that can evaluate your soil. Just make sure they are committed to organic gardening.

portantly, what you like to eat. We have tons of tomatoes, cucumbers for pickling, lettuce for salads, and a wide variety of herbs for seasoning dishes. We also grow broccoli, bell peppers, bush beans, sweet potatoes, cabbage, red and yellow onions, and strawberries—and that's just in our raised bed! We prefer to grow from seeds, and, whenever possible, choose heirloom and organic varieties.

Plant and Seed Selection

Choosing plants for your garden will depend on many variables, including local climate, the type of garden you've chosen (raised bed, container, or pots in a sunny window), and, most im-

What Can I Drink?

At a certain point—probably on a Friday night—you're going to wonder, "So what am I allowed to drink on a Paleo diet?" Your best options will be water and herbal tea, with the occasional coffee, coconut water, kombucha, almond milk, or coconut milk. You can indulge in the rare glass of juice, red wine, or a tequila-based beverage, but if you want to get the most benefits from eating Paleo, you should eliminate alcohol and drinks with sugar (juice and sweetened coffee)—at least until you have completed your first 30 days. The same real-food rules still apply here: Keep everything as clean as possible in terms of ingredients.

Unlimited

-Water and Mineral Water

Water is as basic as it gets. The human body needs it to survive, so without question water should always be your first option when it comes to quenching your thirst. We recommend filtered water, as tap water typically is filled with contaminants.

- Herbal Teas

If you aren't a fan of plain water, try decaffeinated herbal teas, which come in a wide variety of flavors. Herbs and spices steeped in hot water are soothing in the evening and very refreshing when served over ice!

Once a Day

- Kombucha

Kombucha is a raw probiotic drink made by fermenting sweetened tea with a symbiotic colony of bacteria and yeast (SCOBY). These live cultures aid in digestion, cleanse your liver, and boost metabolism. Some claim additional health benefits, including the treatment of cancer and arthritis, as well as symptoms of depression, anxiety, and fibromyalgia. Kombucha is a powerful drink that should be incorporated into everyone's diet, but you really only need a cup a day. Various brands are sold at health food stores, but we encourage you to try brewing your own.

- Coconut Water

Coconut water is full of electrolytes, making it the ideal drink after a heavy workout. Forget Gatorade; coconut water is the healthiest way to rehydrate and replenish after a long run or any kind of sport.

- Coffee

If you do not react negatively to caffeine, coffee can stay on your menu. You can enjoy your morning cup of Joe with a splash of coconut milk or heavy cream. Some people puree it with a bit of unsalted butter from grass-fed cows!

- Almond Milk and Coconut Milk

Beware of strange ingredients in store-bought almond or coconut milk. They may contain filler ingredients as well as sugar. Your best bet is to look for canned, full-fat coconut milk. Or, better yet, make your own nut and coconut milks. It's fairly simple and very rewarding!

Rarely

- 100 Percent Juice

Pure, organic juice is fine every once in a while, but it shouldn't be indulged in every day. Consider how many oranges you need to make one cup of orange juice. That's a lot of sugar in one little cup!

- Raw Milk

Most milk sold in stories is pasteurized, which means it has been heated to kill the bacteria that lives in the guts of sick, toxic, grain-fed feedlot cows. It is a dead food with no real health benefits—in fact, it can cause negative reactions in the body when consumed. Raw milk is a live food that comes from grass-fed cows; it is full of beneficial bacteria that aids in digestion. However, you should only start to drink raw milk again after you have eliminated it from your diet for 30 days. If, at that point, you can tolerate it, then feel free to have raw milk every once in awhile. (Including raw milk in your diet is considered more Primal than Paleo; in the latter case, it would fall in the "80/20" category, which is explained later.)

- Alcohol

There is a time and a place for alcohol, and that's usually when you are celebrating something—a birthday, wedding, or holiday. If you find yourself at an event that involves drinking, use your best judgment. Stay away from any alcohol that contains gluten (sorry folks, no beer), and opt for a glass of red wine, a gluten-free hard cider, or tequila. Avoiding alcohol, especially when everyone else is drinking, may seem like a bummer, but your liver will thank you, and the resulting loss of body fat will definitely be worth it!

Never

Beer is an obvious no-no: It's made with wheat, and wheat is an absolute never on a Paleo diet. And processed, sugary drinks like soda, energy drinks, diet soda, and sweetened beverages fall in the same category, this time because of the sugar they contain. Artificial sugars are no better; they are extremely toxic to the body, and have been linked to cancer. Giving up processed drinks may seem like a big struggle at first, but trust us: After 30 days, you will feel so much better without them!

Unlimited
Water
Mineral Water
Herbal Teas

Rarely
Juice
Raw Milk
Alcohol

Once a Day
Kombucha
Coffee
Coconut Water
Almond and Coconut Milk

Never
Beer
Soda
Energy Drinks
Artificially Flavored
or Sweetened Sodas
and Drinks

Oils and Fats

Healthy fat is an essential component of the Paleo diet; your body depends on it to function properly. Here, we outline the best sources and how they relate to Paleo cooking. All of these oils and fats can be found in local health food stores, online, or in better grocery stores.

Unrefined Virgin Coconut Oil

Coconut oil is solid at room temperature, which makes it perfect for stovetop cooking (like sautéing vegetables and frying eggs) and for any grain-free baking. It does not have an overpowering coconut taste, as you might suspect, and adds wonderful flavor to dishes.

Olive Oil

Olive oil is our primary oil for making salad dressings and marinades. It is liquid at room temperature but will solidify when chilled. Olive oil is not as heat-stable as saturated tropical fats or animal fats, so use it only in cold dishes.

Avocado Oil

Like olive oil, limit this to cold dishes—its creamy flavor is particularly wonderful in salad dressings. Just drizzle it on whatever you are having and add a splash of fresh lemon juice or balsamic vinegar.

Macadamia Nut Oil

This oil is our favorite choice for homemade mayonnaise. Macadamia nut oil has a very mild flavor, with just the slightest hint of sweetness and warmth. You can also use it for a simple salad dressing.

Sesame Oil

Derived from sesame seeds, this oil's distinctive flavor is perfect for Asian dishes. It is not heat-stable, so avoid high-heat applications; use it in salad dressings or as flavoring after cooking.

Red Palm Oil

Red palm oil is virgin and unrefined, which makes it your best choice when purchasing palm oil. Pairing it with dishes can be tricky; we find the distinctive flavor, with its warm undertones, works well with international cuisine. Note: The oil is a rich red and can change the color of food.

Ghee

Ghee is clarified butter, meaning the milk solids (or proteins) have been removed, resulting in pure fat. You can use ghee in place of butter or oil in a recipe. It's available at most health food stores, but it can be easily made at home: Slowly simmer grass-fed butter until the solids have settled at the bottom and a froth has appeared on the top. The ghee is between the top and bottom layers. Carefully remove the froth and spoon out the ghee without disturbing the solids at the bottom.

Grass-Fed Butter (Pastured Butter)

This is another fantastic fat to use in cooking. Butter is labeled "grass-fed" when it is produced from the milk of grass-fed cows. There's really nothing better on steamed vegetables, and it's a good option when sautéing and roasting vegetables, too. We also use it to baste roasted or baked poultry.

Lard

Lard is derived from the fat of pigs. You can easily render your own by saving bacon grease in a glass jar. Store it in the fridge for any time you crave delicious bacon-flavored eggs or vegetables.

Schmaltz

When you see the word "schmaltz" at your local farm stand, it is referring to the Yiddish term for the rendered fat of domestic fowl. Personally, we like to use schmaltz to fry onions and chicken liver. Schmaltz is also fantastic for roasted vegetables, or for basting roasted chicken.

Tallow

Tallow is rendered beef fat and therefore a saturated fat. It is incredibly heat-stable so it is ideal for high-heat cooking. It's an obvious choice for browning meats, but its fairly mild flavor makes it fantastic for cooking any vegetables, too.

Palm Shortening (marketed as Vegetable Shortening)

This is a staple item for all of our grain-free baking recipes because it essentially has no flavor or smell. We often substitute palm shortening for coconut oil in our cookie, piecrust, and muffin recipes.

Coconut Butter

Similar in consistency to nut butters, coconut butter is simply the oil and the meat of the coconut combined. Perfect for sauces, stir-fries, and smoothies. You can also enjoy it with fresh fruit.

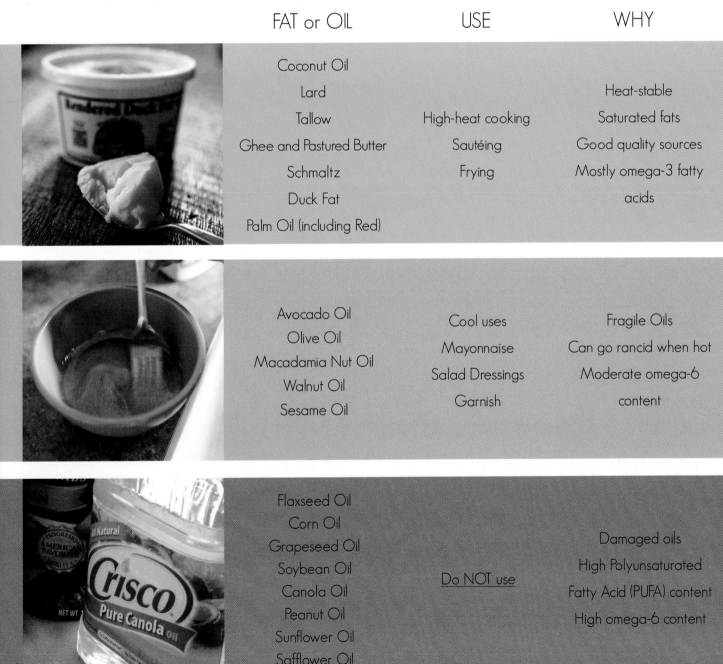

FAT or OIL	USE	WHY
Coconut Oil, Lard, Tallow, Ghee and Pastured Butter, Schmaltz, Duck Fat, Palm Oil (including Red)	High-heat cooking, Sautéing, Frying	Heat-stable, Saturated fats, Good quality sources, Mostly omega-3 fatty acids
Avocado Oil, Olive Oil, Macadamia Nut Oil, Walnut Oil, Sesame Oil	Cool uses, Mayonnaise, Salad Dressings, Garnish	Fragile Oils, Can go rancid when hot, Moderate omega-6 content
Flaxseed Oil, Corn Oil, Grapeseed Oil, Soybean Oil, Canola Oil, Peanut Oil, Sunflower Oil, Safflower Oil	Do NOT use	Damaged oils, High Polyunsaturated Fatty Acid (PUFA) content, High omega-6 content

Nuts and Seeds

Nuts and seeds are a fantastic garnish, as well as a great snack when you are in a pinch. Offering a good amount of protein and fat, a small handful of nuts or seeds can keep hunger at bay for quite some time. To obtain the most nutritional benefit from nuts and seeds, it is best to consume them raw, or, better yet, soak them overnight and then dehydrate them. We use nuts and seeds as a garnish except when it comes to grain-free baking; nut flours and butters make fantastic substitutes for conventional wheat flour.

Add nuts and seeds to salads to enhance flavor and texture, sprinkle over soups, create your own raw trail mix, or grab a small handful when you need a quick energy hit. Here are some of our favorites for snacking and garnishing dishes:

- Almonds
- Walnuts
- Pecans
- Macadamia nuts
- Sunflower seeds
- Flax seeds
- Pine nuts

You can make a nut butter out of any nut you desire. These are great to spread over fruit or vegetables, as well as to add to sauces or dips. Nut butters can create a tasty grain-free treat as well. Our "go-to" nut butters can be made at home, or purchased at your local grocery store or health food store:

- Almond butter
- Sunbutter

Nut flours are a staple ingredient in our grain-free baking recipes, and particularly for cookies, pie crust, pizza crust, and crackers. You won't be doing any baking during your first 30 days on the Paleo diet, but keep this information handy for when you are ready to reward yourself with a treat.

Blanched Almond Flour

The skin of the almond is removed so this nut four is very fine. It's similar to conventional flour and will produce a very smooth-textured baked good.

Almond Meal

With meal the almond's skin is ground into the flour, which produces a coarser texture. You can make almond meal at home by grinding raw almonds in a food processor. It's fine for baking, but if you want flawless results, go with blanched almond flour.

Flax Seed Meal

Flax seed meal is ground flax seeds. We typically use it for more savory recipes, like our "n'oatmeal cookies," pizza crust, and grain-free crackers. You can also sprinkle whole flax seeds over salads, or add to grain-free baked goods to create a more "earthy" flavor.

Pecan Meal

We make this flour at home in our food processor. It's our first choice for piecrusts for our grain-free pumpkin or apple pies.

Herbs and Spices

Fresh herbs and spices bring life to your dishes. We want our dishes to be enhanced by herbs and spices, but not overpowered by them. A little goes a long way, and fresh is always best. To keep waste to a minimum, you can freeze any leftover fresh herbs for future use.

In our recipes, you'll see us use a few classic herbs rather than exotic or hard to find ones. With most dishes we stick to fresh herbs like rosemary, thyme, cilantro, basil, dill, parsley, and sage. These herbs are easy to grow in containers or in a small kitchen garden outside. Rosemary and thyme are "woody" herbs that are hardy in most climates. This means that you can plant them once and enjoy them for many years. Basil, cilantro, parsley, and dill will require annual planting.

To prepare fresh herbs, simply rinse them briefly under cold water, then separate the leaves from the stems. When chopping fresh herbs, you should cut them to the desired size on the first pass—otherwise you'll bruise the leaves. The other preferred method is passing the leaves through an herb mill.

Flavor Pairings

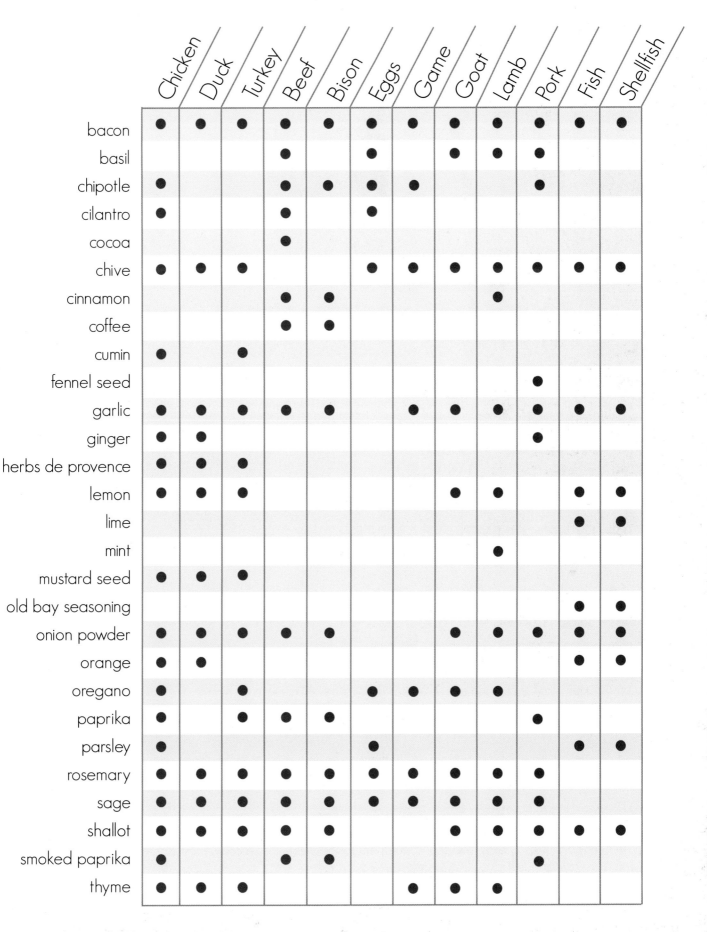

	Chicken	Duck	Turkey	Beef	Bison	Eggs	Game	Goat	Lamb	Pork	Fish	Shellfish
bacon	●	●	●	●	●	●	●	●	●	●	●	●
basil				●	●			●	●	●		
chipotle	●			●	●	●	●			●		
cilantro	●			●		●						
cocoa				●								
chive	●	●	●			●	●	●	●	●	●	●
cinnamon				●	●				●			
coffee				●	●							
cumin	●		●									
fennel seed										●		
garlic	●	●	●	●	●		●	●	●	●	●	●
ginger	●	●								●		
herbs de provence	●	●	●									
lemon	●	●	●					●	●		●	●
lime											●	●
mint									●			
mustard seed	●	●	●									
old bay seasoning											●	●
onion powder	●	●	●	●	●			●	●	●	●	●
orange	●	●									●	●
oregano	●		●			●	●	●	●			
paprika	●		●	●	●					●		
parsley	●					●					●	●
rosemary	●	●	●	●	●	●	●	●	●	●		
sage	●	●	●	●	●	●	●	●	●	●		
shallot	●	●	●	●	●			●	●	●	●	●
smoked paprika	●			●	●					●		
thyme	●	●	●				●	●	●			

Other Key Ingredients

As your palate evolves during your personal Paleo or Primal journey, and as you become more adventurous in the kitchen, you will want to expand your pantry. We like to stock the following ingredients. Some may be a little tricky to find in your local grocery store, but all are available online. You won't need all of these ingredients during your first 30 days, but keep the list on hand for when you start baking treats and sweets. More on that later!

Coconut Aminos

Coconut aminos, which come from the sap of coconut trees, are a less salty, slightly sweeter, and altogether fantastic alternative to soy sauce. We use them in dressings and marinades and to season meat or fish.

Fish Sauce

Fish sauce is a great way to add big flavor to dishes. Be cautious when purchasing it, though, and read labels carefully; many available brands contain sugar or other undesirable ingredients. Your best bet is an extra-virgin fish sauce that contains just fish and salt.

Brown Mustard

We use spicy mustard, or Dijon-style mustard, for dressings, marinades, or steak rubs. When purchasing Dijon-style mustard, always read the ingredients; many contain sugar or wine. When buying brown mustard, look for a brand that contains just mustard seeds, apple cider vinegar, spices, and salt.

Coconut Milk

Coconut milk is essential in a Primal pantry. You can use it as cream in coffee or tea, and add it to sauces, curries, soups, and marinades, as well as in homemade smoothies. Coconut milk is the base for all of our ice cream and pudding recipes, which you can look forward to after you complete your first 30 days. It is available at most grocery stores, but can easily be made at home.

Almond Milk

Like coconut milk, we prefer to make our almond milk from scratch, but you can also purchase it at your local grocery or health food store. Opt for plain and unsweetened to avoid sugar and other undesirable ingredients. Almond milk is fantastic over grain-free granola or in coffee or tea. It can also be added to soups, smoothies, and homemade ice creams.

Unrefined Sea Salt

When eliminating processed foods from your diet, you will automatically be eliminating a lot of sodium. We use salt sparingly, and only during cooking; we rarely add it to a dish after it has been cooked. However you use it, always choose an unrefined natural sea salt. This will add fantastic flavor to your dishes minus the chemicals of processed salts.

Broths and Stocks

Bone broths and stocks are easy to make on your own, and a great way to bring minerals and nutrients into your diet. Nothing quite says comfort like a hot cup of homemade stock. We encourage you to always make broth from scratch, because this is a real food. Processed soup broth or stock is never ideal, but the Imagine Organics brand is fine in a pinch. We generally use a pressure cooker, which is the fastest way to make homemade broth.

Dehydrated Unsweetened Coconut (flaked or shredded)

This is perfect as a fast and nutritious add to trail mix, or simply as a snack on its own. You will find shredded coconut in a few of our grain-free baked recipes, but dehydrated coconut is delicious in savory dishes as well.

Almond Flour and Coconut Flour

Almond flour is our favorite option for grain-free baking. It's great for cookies, crackers, breads, cakes, muffins, and cupcakes. For those with nut allergies, coconut flour is usually a good substitute and our top choice for fluffy, cake-like desserts. You can also use it as a binder in crab cakes or meatballs, as breading for shrimp or chicken, and to thicken sauces or gravies. It's pretty dense, so a little goes a long way.

Vinegars

We do not use vinegars often, but they are fine in moderation to flavor dressings and marinades. Unfiltered and raw apple cider vinegar is the healthiest choice, however the smell and flavor is very strong. We also include balsamic, white balsamic, and raspberry balsamic vinegars in our recipes, but you can easily replace any vinegar with the fresh juice of a lemon or lime.

Step One: A Total Junk Food Purge!

So here you are, ready to embark on your journey to total health. We're about to give you your meal plans, shopping lists, and recipes. You're ready, right? Not quite. Before you can fill your kitchen with a bounty of fresh, nutritious food, you need to dump all the junk that's clogging your cupboards and fridge. And we're going to make this first, critical step very easy for you: Throw it all out!

Start by tossing opened or expired products. Food that is new or cans that are unopened can be donated to a local food pantry or homeless shelter. Does that sound like a waste of food? Sure, if you're defining food as anything edible. Most of the stuff you'll be throwing out is completely devoid of nutritional value. So get rid of it....like, now!

Until you are rock solid in your commitment to your new lifestyle, you are in danger of cheating. Disposing of easy temptations—bags of chips, boxes of crackers and cookies, that jar of peanut butter—dramatically increases your chance of success. That's why they need to go this minute, no ifs, ands, or buts.

We know what you're thinking: What if I don't like Paleo? I will want those foods back. Truthfully, that mentality only sets you up for failure. Toss those thoughts in the garbage along with junk food! You will be fine, we promise. In 30 days, what seems like a sacrifice now will look like the greatest gift you ever gave yourself.

Foods to permanently eliminate:

- All grains (wheat, rice, corn)
- Cereal, crackers, cookies, cakes
- Anything with soy in it
- Seed oils (canola oil, safflower oil)
- All soda
- All candy
- Artificial sweeteners
- Peanut products
- Food dyes and colorings
- Overly processed, chemical-laden foods
- Beer
- Genetically modified foods

Foods to eliminate for the first 30 days (you can reintroduce them later on a limited basis)

- Alcohol
- White potatoes
- Juice
- Natural sweeteners and sugars (including too much fruit)
- Chocolate (including dark)
- Dried fruits
- Grain-free, Paleo treats

Meal Building 101

Before we get into the nitty-gritty of meal building, let's define a few of the common terms.

Paleo

Building a Paleo meal is simple when you are prepared. That means having the right ingredients and properly prepared foods at your fingertips. After years of consuming carbohydrates—grains, sugar, and processed foods—your body has become adapted to storing fat rather than burning it. With the Paleo diet, you will be switching over to burning fat through the eating of plants, animals, and healthy fats (also known as being "fat-adapted"). But it can take a little time for that adjustment to happen, and in the meantime, you may need more frequent meals or snacks. That's fine. Just be sure to have healthy choices available at home, at work, or wherever you are, which requires a bit of planning. Don't worry: Once your body switches over to a more efficient system, you will be able to go for much longer periods of time between meals.

You might be thinking, *I know what I can and can't eat, but how much can I eat?* That depends on a few things: your size, your activity level, and how hungry you are. Here's an example of a classic Paleo meal that works for just about everyone. Fill a big bowl with colorful vegetables (you can pretty much eat unlimited amounts of veggies), top with your choice of meat (the equivalent of what fits in the palm of your hand), dress with healthy fat (just enough olive oil, avocado oil, or macadamia nut oil to lightly coat your ingredients), and add lemon juice or vinegar for flavor. Can't get much simpler than that, right?

[A typical Paleo/Primal breakfast for two]

Primal

We've briefly discussed Primal, which is very similar to Paleo. The few, simple differences are that Primal allows for the consumption of more saturated fats and good quality full-fat dairy from pastured cows or goats.

[A typical Paleo lunch or dinner]

A Primal meal will look very similar to a Paleo meal, except you may see a garnish of raw, grass-fed cheese added to the plate, heavy cream in coffee or a recipe, and the use of grass-fed butter in cooking. Typically, when first adopting a Paleo or Primal diet, it is best to use your first month to eliminate all possible food irritants. These can then be reintroduced after 30 days. If you find, for example, that you can toler-

ate full-fat dairy, then Primal will be a good fit. If you find that you are bloated, gassy, have skin breakouts, gain weight, or feel depressed, then avoid it.

This way of eating is all about being aware and listening to your body. But that's not always possible; a lifetime of eating processed foods means you've built up a tolerance to toxins and irritants. Think of them as noise drowning everything else out; before you can hear what your body needs, you have to clear out the toxins with a 30-day detox.

Gluten-Free

"Gluten-free" is one of the biggest trends in food right now. But what exactly does it mean? The simplest answer is that you are not including any gluten-containing grains in your diet. Gluten is the protein found in wheat, barley, and rye, and it causes a host of health issues for many people. The most common illness associated with gluten intolerance is Celiac Disease, but anyone can react negatively to gluten. Switching to gluten-free grains is an option. Just do your research and be sure to read food labels. Plenty of gluten-free products are processed and should be avoided. Keep in mind, too, that legumes (beans) and grains such as rice, oats, and corn, contain lectins—proteins that are similar to gluten—and can cause symptoms similar to gluten intolerance: fatigue, depression, irritation to the gut, and inflammation in the form of weight gain, breakouts, and rashes (to name a few). This is why it is essential to eliminate all grains during your first 30 days of Paleo eating.

[A *healthy* gluten-free meal can still look a lot like a Paleo meal, but may include starchier options such as peeled and cooked white potatoes.]

What About Snacks?

People who eat Paleo aren't burning sugar anymore to fuel their bodies so they don't snack as much. But we get that there are times when you need a small bite rather than a full meal, or a quick hit of energy to keep you going, especially in the first week or so of your new diet. Have the following on hand so you don't panic when hunger hits.

Our favorite snacks:
- Homemade jerky
- Homemade nut butter with fruit
- Hard-boiled eggs
- A cup of berries, or piece of fruit
- Raw veggies with zucchini hummus
- A small serving of leftovers from a previous meal

Traveling can be particularly stressful: Unless you cook ahead of time, you aren't going to find much at the airport or on the highway. At those times we opt for Steve's PaleoGoods. Steve offers an array of jerky flavor combinations, nuts, and berries, as well as just jerky packs, packs for kids, and bigger packs for athletes. Thanks to Paleo Kits, we always have an option for a healthy snack when we need it most!

Now that you understand the differences between Paleo, Primal, and gluten- free, and you know how to structure a meal, you are ready to get cooking!

Shopping Guidelines and Tips

For most people, the idea of going to the grocery store is tedious, but not for us: It's one of our favorite activities! We sometimes refer to Whole Foods as our "Happy Place," and we really do consider it just that. We're happy because we know we're shopping for food that will fuel our bodies, taste amazing, and keep us healthy and strong.

The only thing we love more than going to the grocery store is growing and picking our own produce. If there is something we cannot grow, and assuming it's in season, we seek it out at one of the many local farmers' markets. If what we need isn't in our garden or at a market, we hit the grocery store.

Food shopping is creative and relaxing for us. Generally we shop for the entire week. Sometimes we'll see produce that is in season, or a cut of meat from a local farmer that looks amazing, and that will inspire us to create a new recipe. Before you hit the store for inspiration, here are a couple of general shopping rules:

Read the ingredients. Most of what we purchase at the grocery store is fresh, but there are times when we need packaged foods, like brown mustard, canned tomato sauce, canned coconut milk, or nut butter. We never buy a product without checking the ingredients first. If there is anything on the label that looks strange or that we can't pronounce, we do not buy it. In general, we try to choose packaged foods with 5 ingredients or less. The fewer the better!

Meats: If possible, always opt for pasture-raised or grass-fed. We mentioned it before, but it bears repeating—animals are supposed to range freely in pastures, grazing on grasses and soaking up sunlight. They do not thrive on grains, which are used to fatten them up quickly. (Hmmm. Do you think maybe grains fatten up people, too? We think yes.) Unfortunately, not only does the grain make the animals fat, it is full of toxins that make them sick. Those toxins are stored in fat cells, which is why consuming a fatty cut of meat from an animal that was raised on grains is just as unhealthy for you. Grass-fed animals are healthy, lean, and vibrant. Their fat cells are clean, and full of healing omega-3 fatty acids. The meat from grass-fed cattle is also a wonderful source of CLA (conjugated linoleic acid), which the animals obtain from the grasses they eat. Grass-fed organic meats can be pricey, though, so if you can't spare the money, opt for leaner cuts of meat and get your healthy fats from coconut oil, grass-fed butter, olive oil, or avocados.

Seafood: Think of fish as you do meat. If you can afford it, opt for wild-caught. These fish are healthier and full of omega-3 fatty acids. Farmed fish are as sick and toxic as grain-fed animals.

Vegetables and Fruits: Shopping for organic fruits and vegetables can get pricey. One way to keep the cost low is to purchase produce that is in season, or from a local farmers' market. Of course, if you have the means, then growing your own vegetables will give you the biggest bang for your buck. You will know exactly where your produce came from, it will be in season, and there is nothing quite as rewarding as eating food grown by your own two hands. Another way to save on cost, as well as support local agriculture, is to sign up for a CSA.

Fats: This is one item on your list that you should not skimp on. Fats fuel our bodies, feed our brains, and nourish our cells. You want to make sure that you are buying the best quality fats available, and then you need to use them properly. Saturated fats such as grass-fed butter, coconut oil, pastured animal fats, and ghee are the safest to cook with because they do not become damaged when heated. Monounsaturated fats, like olive oil, do become damaged when heated; save them for cold uses, like salad dressings. Polyunsaturated

fats (PUFAs) are the most dangerous to cook with; they contain omega-6 fatty acids, which go rancid when heated! Most nut and seed oils—corn, peanut, sunflower, safflower, etc.—are PUFAs.

Nuts and Seeds:
The consumption of nuts and seeds can be confusing to a Paleo newbie. Contrary to what you may think, they should not be a staple in your diet. Think of them as a garnish or a snack to tide you over. Nuts are fairly high in omega-6 fatty acids, which can cause inflammation and gut irritation. And since we now know that omega-6 fats go rancid when heated, it's best to consume nuts and seeds raw. Nuts are also high in calories, which can cause weight gain, or stall weight loss.

- **Eat pasture-raised meat.** Pastured animal meat is the healthiest form of protein to consume because those animals were raised properly and fed the diet they are supposed to eat. A healthy animal means a healthy you. The same goes for seafood: fresh, wild-caught is best; avoid farmed fish.

- **Shop in season** for locally grown produce, try to find a good farmers' market near you, join a CSA, or grow your own!

- **Don't skimp on fats.** Always choose organic, unrefined oils, and only cook with heat-stable saturated fats. Avoid refined oils high in omega-6 fatty acids, also known as PUFAs.

- **Nuts and seeds should be considered a garnish,** not to be relied upon for frequent snacking, and are best consumed raw.

Just Remember:
- **Always read the ingredients,** and avoid any food item that has too many or strange ingredients, chemicals, sugars, food dyes, etc.

Answers to Common Questions

As you begin your new journey you will naturally have lots of questions, or will have to answer lots of questions from concerned family members and friends. We highlight and answer some of the most common in the following pages. For more in-depth answers, we encourage you to visit Mark Sisson's website, Mark'sDailyApple.com, or Chris Kresser's website, ChrisKresser.com. They are both amazing resources for Primal lifestyle information!

Gluten

Gluten is the protein found in wheat, barley, and rye. The capital offense of gluten is that it can irritate and damage the lining of the small intestine because proteins enter the blood stream before they can be broken down. This is known as leaky gut, and can lead to significant health problems, like Celiac Disease. But, truthfully, most people have some degree of gluten sensitivity, which manifests in a variety of ways—anything from eczema, digestive upset, skin breakouts, and mental health issues like anxiety and depression.

Beyond digestive tract disruption, the high carbohydrate density of most grains and wheat products upset the blood glucose balance in the body. Spikes of insulin lead to a roller coaster of energy throughout the day. That "2 o'clock feeling," or slump, is from eating sandwiches, pasta, or pizza at lunch. A balanced Paleo meal of meat and vegetables will save you from a blood sugar crash later in the day.

Complex Carbohydrates

To add insult to injury, the complex carbs (another way of saying "many sugars") found in most grains are a quick and easy source of energy for the body—and by that we do not mean a good source of energy. Your body needs quick and easy sugar molecules for energy so that it can store away proteins and fats for later use. By eating significant amounts of carbs (sugars), your body stores more complex food molecules as fat. But you do need carbs and energy, so how do you get them in the Paleo diet? From fruits and vegetables, of course. Your body gets all the carbs it needs from a diet rich in plants.

For more information on gluten, read *The New York Times* bestseller *Wheat Belly*, by Dr. William Davis.

Soy

In its traditionally prepared form, fermented soy is not evil; in fact, it's okay. However, in today's world of corporate farming operations, it has become one of the most genetically modified foods (also known as GMOs). Soy is extremely processed—first through acid washing and neutralizing solutions, then as it is formed into fake foods that approximate the real thing (tofurkey anyone?). Soy mimics estrogen in the body, which is linked to tumors in the breasts and uterus. Soy also significantly slows thyroid function and is linked to thyroid cancer. So the soy we typically have access to is not a health food at all, which is why it is best to completely avoid it.

For more details on this subject, read "Soy Scrutiny" at MarksDailyApple.com.

Cholesterol

This necessary hormone has been getting a bad rap since the 1950s. Cholesterol is not only a basic cellular building block; it acts to synthesize vitamins and steroid hormones. We live in a toxic world, full of environmental poisons, chemically treated foods, and life stressors, which cause inflammation and oxidative stress, two primary heart disease indicators. To fight both, you need to fuel your body with whole, nutrient-dense foods, healthy fats, organic vegetables, and pastured meats. The Paleo diet is an anti-inflammatory diet, which is why it's your best first step in avoiding disease.

For more information on the importance of cholesterol in the diet, visit www.chriskresser.com.

The Scoop on Fats

Proper fat intake is critical to your health. With the Paleo diet, you will be stressing healing omega-3 fats and avoiding unhealthy fats high in omega-6 (the fats that kill). Saturated fats are essential because they are heat-stable, fuel our brains, and help our bodies release stored fat once sugar and grains are removed from our diets. Here are the fats you need to avoid: Trans fats, because they are a chemically changed "food" that our bodies are incapable of processing; hydrogenated oils, which are mostly in processed junk food but sometimes hidden in Paleo-approved foods (another good reason to read food labels); and polyunsaturated fats, like canola, safflower, sunflower, and grapeseed oils, which go rancid when heated.

Damaged fats cause inflammation, which makes them extremely harmful to our bodies. Other than saturated fats, we recommend including monounsaturated fats, like avocado and olive oil, in cold dishes; just don't use them cook with, as they, too, become damaged when heated.

Calcium

This is one of the biggest questions you will get: Without dairy, where will you get sufficient calcium? Not to worry: There are plenty of non-dairy sources of calcium in the foods you will be eating. Two servings per day of a fish like sardines, or dark leafy greens, and of course gut-healing bone broth, provide all the calcium you will need, in addition to providing benefits well beyond cal-

cium. And don't forget weight-bearing exercise: Lifting heavy things is a great way to build and maintain strong bones!

For more information on calcium and the Paleo diet, visit: http://chriskresser.com/calcium-supplements-why-you-should-think-twice.

Kale and other dark leafy greens (like broccoli and chard) are good non-dairy sources of calcium.

The "80/20 Rule"

If you follow food or fitness blogs, you've probably read about the "80/20 rule." The thinking behind it is pretty simple: If you eat a strict diet of wholesome, nutritious, organic food 80 percent of the time, you can cheat 20 percent of the time. It's a nice idea, but it won't work if you're looking for results. If your 20 percent is going out with friends and eating pizza and drinking beer on the weekends, or indulging in a pastry or pasta once a week, you will not be eating a Paleo or Primal diet. Far from it, actually! Following such a diet means that 80 percent of the time your meals are good quality meats, organic vegetables, and healthy fats; your 20 percent would be "cheating" with grain-free desserts and grass-fed dairy products, if you can tolerate them. Believe us when we say that this is the only way to get your digestive system functioning properly so that you can properly absorb all the nutrients your body needs.

For us, the ratio is more like 95/5. That may sound fanatical or impossible if you are just beginning to eat Paleo, but you will be amazed at how your cravings for sugar and bad fats diminish once your body has detoxified. If you go to our website or read our other cookbooks, you will find plenty of recipes for grain-free treats sweetened with maple syrup, honey and dates; we enjoy them as much as anyone. Indulging 5 percent of the time is plenty when your body is working the way it should.

This coffee cake from *Gather*, our second cookbook, would be considered an 80/20 treat.

What is "Strict Paleo"?

In a nutshell, it's eating just the basics: meat, veggies, healthy fats, fruits, nuts and seeds. Each meal should contain a serving of protein, lots of colorful veggies, and a garnish of healthy fat. Once you have adjusted to this new lifestyle, and your blood sugar regulates, you won't feel the need to snack so much, though raw nuts and fruit are a fine, light snack or treat now and then. Always focus on meat, veggies, and healthy fats and you will have success on a Paleo diet—not only that, you will start feeling better than ever! A strict Paleo diet does not include any grain-free baked treats—that would be considered "80/20" Paleo. Limit those foods to special occasions or gatherings with friends and family.

Part 2
30 Day Meal Plan

{ Designed for Two People }

We've created your 30-day meal plan to set you up for success in your first month of following the Paleo diet—to guide you every step of the way! To get you started, we've compiled a shopping list of the kitchen staples and basic ingredients used in most of our recipes (next page).

The meal plan is broken down week by week. Each week includes a detailed calendar of the suggested meals, plus shopping lists. If you like to experiment in the kitchen, you can follow the plan's guidelines and create your own recipes. Similarly, if you find you prefer some of the recipes, you can substitute them for the ones you don't like as much. This is the way we cook at home, and a method for streamlining the Paleo lifestyle.

The meal plan is designed to feed two people. Some recipes are family-size and intended to be used for multiple meals or leftovers. If you are an experienced cook, feel free to adjust quantities (the shopping lists, however, display the quantities in the recipes). The meal plan is intended as a general guideline. You can choose to prepare any recipe for any meal. There are no rules. We have provided a road map, but you are free to take detours.

the 30 Day Guide to Paleo Cooking

Basic Ingredients

Nuts & Seeds

- [ ] Almonds, whole and slivered
- [ ] Macadamia nuts
- [ ] Pecans
- [ ] Pine nuts
- [ ] Walnuts

Produce

- [ ] Avocado
- [ ] Garlic
- [ ] Kalamata olives
- [ ] Lemons
- [ ] Limes

Oils & Fats

- [ ] Avocado oil
- [ ] Butter, grass-fed
- [ ] Coconut oil
- [ ] Duck fat or lard
- [ ] Ghee
- [ ] Macadamia nut oil
- [ ] Olive oil, extra-virgin
- [ ] Red palm oil
- [ ] Sesame oil
- [ ] Tallow
- [ ] Toasted sesame oil

Dried Spices

- [ ] Basil
- [ ] Black pepper
- [ ] Bay leaves
- [ ] Cayenne
- [ ] Chipotle powder
- [ ] Chinese 5-spice
- [ ] Cinnamon
- [ ] Coriander
- [ ] Cumin
- [ ] Curry
- [ ] Dill
- [ ] Fennel seeds
- [ ] Garam masala
- [ ] Garlic powder
- [ ] Ginger
- [ ] Marjoram
- [ ] Nutmeg
- [ ] Onion powder
- [ ] Old Bay seasoning
- [ ] Oregano
- [ ] Paprika
- [ ] Pumpkin pie spice
- [ ] Red pepper flakes
- [ ] Rosemary
- [ ] Sage (rubbed)

- [ ] Salt (sea & truffle)
- [ ] Sesame seeds
- [ ] Smoked paprika
- [ ] Thyme
- [ ] Turmeric
- [ ] White pepper

Vinegars

- [ ] Apple cider vinegar
- [ ] Balsamic vinegar
- [ ] White balsamic vinegar

Other

- [ ] Capers
- [ ] Chicken stock
- [ ] Coconut aminos
- [ ] Coconut milk
- [ ] Fish sauce
- [ ] Spicy brown mustard
- [ ] _____
- [ ] _____
- [ ] _____
- [ ] _____
- [ ] _____

Week 1 Meal Plan

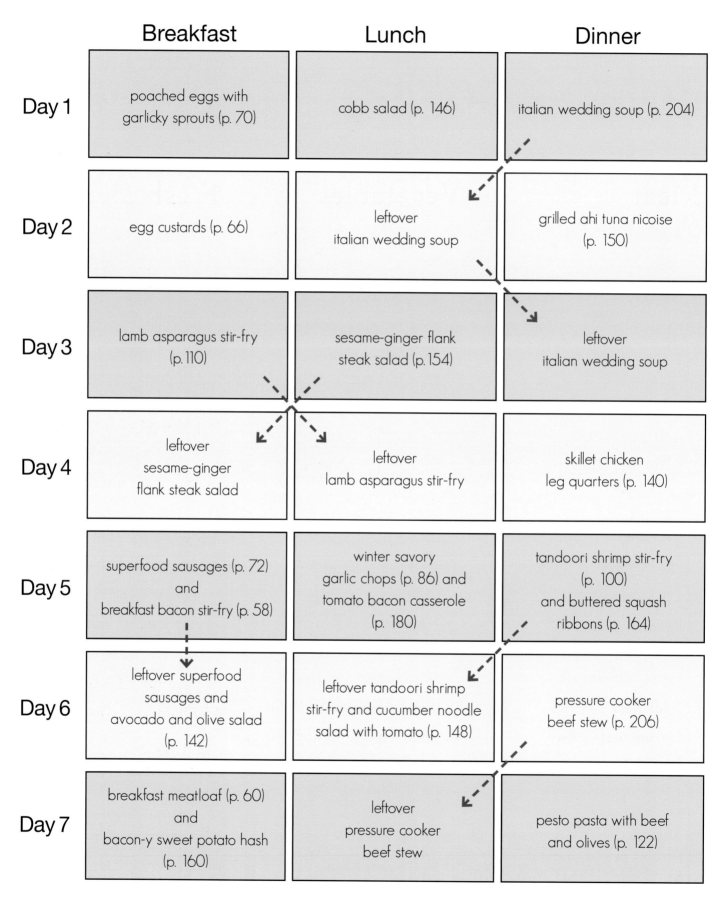

	Breakfast	Lunch	Dinner
Day 1	poached eggs with garlicky sprouts (p. 70)	cobb salad (p. 146)	italian wedding soup (p. 204)
Day 2	egg custards (p. 66)	leftover italian wedding soup	grilled ahi tuna nicoise (p. 150)
Day 3	lamb asparagus stir-fry (p. 110)	sesame-ginger flank steak salad (p. 154)	leftover italian wedding soup
Day 4	leftover sesame-ginger flank steak salad	leftover lamb asparagus stir-fry	skillet chicken leg quarters (p. 140)
Day 5	superfood sausages (p. 72) and breakfast bacon stir-fry (p. 58)	winter savory garlic chops (p. 86) and tomato bacon casserole (p. 180)	tandoori shrimp stir-fry (p. 100) and buttered squash ribbons (p. 164)
Day 6	leftover superfood sausages and avocado and olive salad (p. 142)	leftover tandoori shrimp stir-fry and cucumber noodle salad with tomato (p. 148)	pressure cooker beef stew (p. 206)
Day 7	breakfast meatloaf (p. 60) and bacon-y sweet potato hash (p. 160)	leftover pressure cooker beef stew	pesto pasta with beef and olives (p. 122)

the 30 Day Guide to Paleo Cooking

Week 1
Shopping List

Meat

- [ ] Ahi tuna steak (day 2) - 1 (8 oz) steak
- [ ] Bacon - 2 lbs
- [ ] Beef bone broth (2 lbs beef marrow bones) – 6 cups, re-serving one additional cup and freezing for a Week 2 recipe
- [ ] Beef liver - ½ lb
- [ ] Beef stew meat - 3 lbs
- [ ] Chicken bone broth (1 chicken back & neck) - 8 cups
- [ ] Chicken leg quarters - 2
- [ ] Chicken tenders - ½ lb
- [ ] Chops (lamb, goat or pork) - 4 chops
- [ ] Eggs - 2 dozen
- [ ] Flank steak - 1 ½ lbs
- [ ] Ground beef - 2 lbs
- [ ] Ground lamb (or beef) - 1 lb
- [ ] Ground pork - 4 lbs
- [ ] Ham - ½ cup cubed
- [ ] Shrimp, peeled, and de-veined (day 5) - 1 ½ lbs

Vegetables

- [ ] Asparagus – 2 ½ lbs
- [ ] Broccoli - 1 head
- [ ] Brussels sprouts - 2 cups
- [ ] Cabbage - 1 large, or 2 medium
- [ ] Carrots - 1 lb
- [ ] Celery - 1 head
- [ ] Cucumber- 3 medium
- [ ] Escarole - 1 head
- [ ] Green beans, french-style - 1 cup
- [ ] Green leaf lettuce - 2 heads
- [ ] Red bell peppers - 3
- [ ] Red potatoes - 4 small
- [ ] Shitake mushrooms - 2 cups
- [ ] Spaghetti squash - 2 large
- [ ] Spring mix salad greens - 9 cups
- [ ] Sweet potatoes - 3 large
- [ ] White mushrooms - 2 cups
- [ ] Yellow onions - 5 medium
- [ ] Yellow squash - 1 medium
- [ ] Zucchini - 2 medium

Fresh Herbs

- [ ] Basil - 1 large bunch
- [ ] Chives - 2 Tbsp
- [ ] Cilantro - ½ cup
- [ ] Oregano - 3 Tbsp
- [ ] Savory - 5 sprigs

Fruit

- [ ] Tomatoes - 1 Roma, 4 vine, 2 medium yellow, 2 cups grape tomatoes

Other

- [ ] Black sea salt to garnish (optional) - 2 Tbsp
- [ ] Diced tomatoes, no salt added - 1 can (15 oz)
- [ ] Pine nuts - 1/3 cup
- [ ] Tandoori - 1 Tbsp

Additional

- [ ] _____
- [ ] _____
- [ ] _____
- [ ] _____

Week 2 Meal Plan

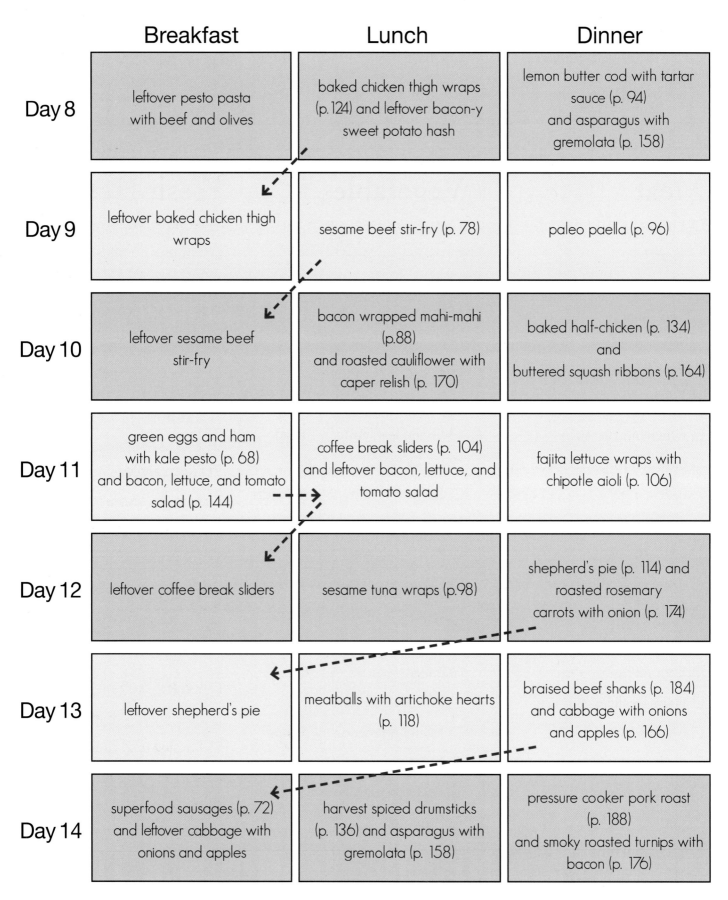

	Breakfast	Lunch	Dinner
Day 8	leftover pesto pasta with beef and olives	baked chicken thigh wraps (p. 124) and leftover bacon-y sweet potato hash	lemon butter cod with tartar sauce (p. 94) and asparagus with gremolata (p. 158)
Day 9	leftover baked chicken thigh wraps	sesame beef stir-fry (p. 78)	paleo paella (p. 96)
Day 10	leftover sesame beef stir-fry	bacon wrapped mahi-mahi (p.88) and roasted cauliflower with caper relish (p. 170)	baked half-chicken (p. 134) and buttered squash ribbons (p. 164)
Day 11	green eggs and ham with kale pesto (p. 68) and bacon, lettuce, and tomato salad (p. 144)	coffee break sliders (p. 104) and leftover bacon, lettuce, and tomato salad	fajita lettuce wraps with chipotle aioli (p. 106)
Day 12	leftover coffee break sliders	sesame tuna wraps (p.98)	shepherd's pie (p. 114) and roasted rosemary carrots with onion (p. 174)
Day 13	leftover shepherd's pie	meatballs with artichoke hearts (p. 118)	braised beef shanks (p. 184) and cabbage with onions and apples (p. 166)
Day 14	superfood sausages (p. 72) and leftover cabbage with onions and apples	harvest spiced drumsticks (p. 136) and asparagus with gremolata (p. 158)	pressure cooker pork roast (p. 188) and smoky roasted turnips with bacon (p. 176)

the 30 Day Guide to Paleo Cooking

Week 2
Shopping List

Meat

- ☐ Bacon - 1 lb
- ☐ Beef liver - ½ lb
- ☐ Beef shanks - 4 shanks
- ☐ Beef (steak) - 3 lbs
- ☐ Chicken - ½ of whole chicken
- ☐ Chicken breast, boneless and skinless - ½ lb
- ☐ Chicken drumsticks - 12
- ☐ Chicken thighs, bone in and skin on - 8
- ☐ Cod filet (day 8) - 1 lb
- ☐ Eggs - 4
- ☐ Flank steak - ½ lb
- ☐ Ground beef, pork or lamb - 2 lbs
- ☐ Ground pork - 3 lbs
- ☐ Ham - 6 slices
- ☐ Mahi-Mahi (day 10) - 1 ½ lbs
- ☐ Pork roast - 3-4 lbs
- ☐ Shrimp, peeled and deveined (day 9) - ½ lb
- ☐ Yellowtail tuna (day 12) - ¾ lb

Vegetables

- ☐ Artichoke hearts - 2 cups
- ☐ Asparagus - 4 lbs
- ☐ Carrots - 3 lbs
- ☐ Cauliflower - 4 heads
- ☐ Celery - 1 bunch
- ☐ Cucumber - ½ cup
- ☐ Green cabbage - 2 heads
- ☐ Green leaf lettuce - 1 head
- ☐ Green onion - 2 sprigs
- ☐ Iceberg lettuce - 2 large heads
- ☐ Kale - 2 cups
- ☐ Red bell peppers - 3
- ☐ Shiitake mushrooms - 2 cups
- ☐ Spaghetti squash - 1 medium
- ☐ Spring mix salad greens - 2 cups
- ☐ Turnips - 4 medium
- ☐ White mushrooms - 3 cups
- ☐ Yellow onions - 8 medium
- ☐ Yellow squash - 3 medium
- ☐ Zucchini - 3 medium

Fresh Herbs

- ☐ Basil - ½ cup
- ☐ Cilantro - 1 Tbsp
- ☐ Flat leaf parsley - 3 large bunches
- ☐ Fresh oregano - 2 Tbsp
- ☐ Thyme - 1 bunch

Fruit

- ☐ Green apples - 2
- ☐ Kumato (brown tomato) - 1
- ☐ Vine ripened tomatoes - 2

Other

- ☐ Coffee, finely ground - 1 Tbsp
- ☐ Pickles - 2 Tbsp
- ☐ Pine nuts - ⅓ cup
- ☐ Roasted nori sheets
- ☐ Saffron - 4 strands
- ☐ Water chestnuts - ½ cup

Week 3 Meal Plan

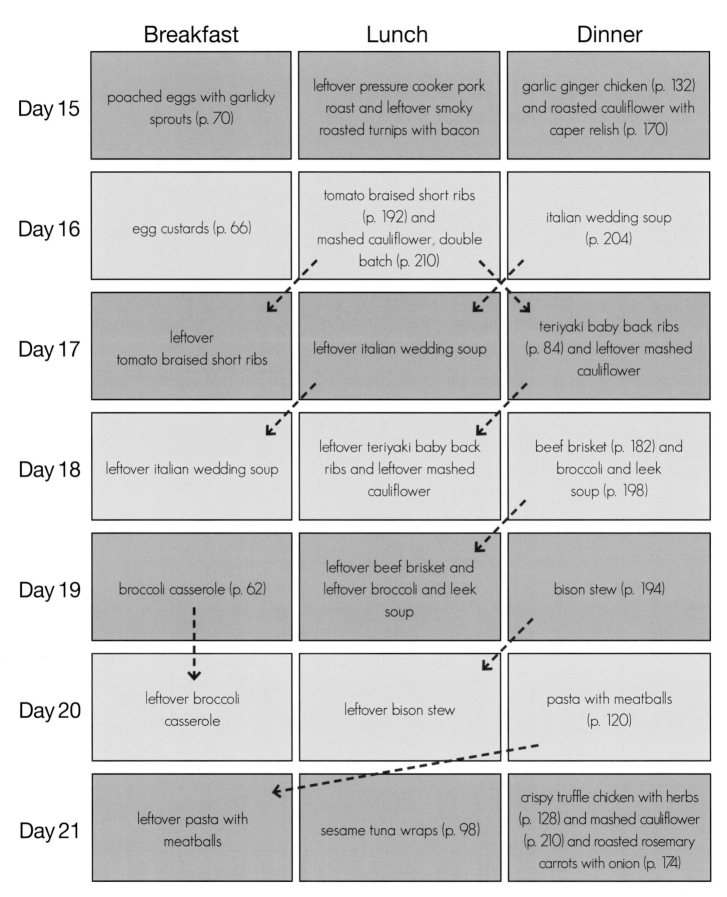

	Breakfast	Lunch	Dinner
Day 15	poached eggs with garlicky sprouts (p. 70)	leftover pressure cooker pork roast and leftover smoky roasted turnips with bacon	garlic ginger chicken (p. 132) and roasted cauliflower with caper relish (p. 170)
Day 16	egg custards (p. 66)	tomato braised short ribs (p. 192) and mashed cauliflower, double batch (p. 210)	italian wedding soup (p. 204)
Day 17	leftover tomato braised short ribs	leftover italian wedding soup	teriyaki baby back ribs (p. 84) and leftover mashed cauliflower
Day 18	leftover italian wedding soup	leftover teriyaki baby back ribs and leftover mashed cauliflower	beef brisket (p. 182) and broccoli and leek soup (p. 198)
Day 19	broccoli casserole (p. 62)	leftover beef brisket and leftover broccoli and leek soup	bison stew (p. 194)
Day 20	leftover broccoli casserole	leftover bison stew	pasta with meatballs (p. 120)
Day 21	leftover pasta with meatballs	sesame tuna wraps (p. 98)	crispy truffle chicken with herbs (p. 128) and mashed cauliflower (p. 210) and roasted rosemary carrots with onion (p. 174)

the 30 Day Guide to Paleo Cooking

Week 3 Shopping List

Meat

- ☐ Bacon - ½ lb
- ☐ Beef bone broth (2 lbs beef marrow bones) - 8 cups, reserving 2 cups to freeze for a Week 4 recipe
- ☐ Beef brisket - 2 lbs
- ☐ Beef short ribs - 5 lbs
- ☐ Bison steak medallions (stew meat) - 2 lbs
- ☐ Chicken thighs - 8
- ☐ Chicken stock (2 chicken backs & necks – 2 batches) - 13 cups
- ☐ Chicken, whole - 6 lbs
- ☐ Eggs - 15
- ☐ Ground pork - 5 lbs
- ☐ Pork baby back ribs - 3 lbs
- ☐ _____
- ☐ _____
- ☐ _____
- ☐ _____
- ☐ _____

Vegetables

- ☐ Broccoli - 4 heads
- ☐ Brussels sprouts - 2 cups
- ☐ Carrots - 2 lbs
- ☐ Cauliflower - 5 heads
- ☐ Celery - 1 bunch
- ☐ Escarole - 1 head
- ☐ Green onion (garnish) - ¼ cup
- ☐ Leek - 1 stalk
- ☐ Spaghetti squash - 1 medium
- ☐ White mushrooms - 5 cups
- ☐ Yellow onions - 5 medium
- ☐ _____
- ☐ _____
- ☐ _____
- ☐ _____

Fresh Herbs

- ☐ Chives - 2 Tbsp
- ☐ Fresh ginger root - 1 Tbsp
- ☐ Thyme - 3 sprigs
- ☐ Rosemary - 3 sprigs

Other

- ☐ Black olives - ¼ cup
- ☐ Strained tomatoes - 2 cups
- ☐ Tomato paste - 1 small can (6 oz)
- ☐ Tomato sauce (Muir Glen, no salt added) - 3 cans, 15 oz each

Additional

- ☐ _____
- ☐ _____
- ☐ _____
- ☐ _____
- ☐ _____
- ☐ _____
- ☐ _____
- ☐ _____

Week 4 Meal Plan

	Breakfast	Lunch	Dinner
Day 22	green eggs and ham with kale pesto (p. 68) and almond flour pancakes (p. 56)	leftover crispy truffle chicken with herbs and leftover mashed cauliflower and leftover roasted rosemary carrots with onion	paleo paella (p. 96)
Day 23	lamb chops two ways (p. 76)	pesto pasta with beef and olives (p. 122)	coffee-marinated flat iron steaks (p. 64) and bacon, lettuce, and tomato salad (p. 144)
Day 24	leftover coffee-marinated flat iron steaks and leftover bacon, lettuce and tomato salad	leftover pesto pasta with beef and olives	rump roast under pressure (p. 190) and cream of mushroom soup (p. 202)
Day 25	leftover rump roast under pressure and leftover cream of mushroom soup	cobb salad (p. 146)	garlic and dill sockeye salmon (p. 92) and mashed cauliflower (p. 210)
Day 26	leftover garlic and dill sockeye salmon and leftover mashed cauliflower	chicken soup with bone broth (p. 200)	skillet chicken leg quarters (p. 140)
Day 27	leftover chicken soup with bone broth	cherry balsamic pasta (p. 116)	grilled ahi tuna nicoise (p. 150)
Day 28	egg custards (p. 66)	leftover cherry balsamic pasta	meatloaf (p. 112) and smoky roasted turnips with bacon (p. 176)
Day 29	leftover meatloaf and leftover smoky roasted turnips with bacon	sesame-ginger flank steak salad (p. 154)	duck a l'orange (p. 130) and cucumber noodle salad with tomato (p. 148)
Day 30	leftover sesame-ginger flank steak salad	leftover duck a l'orange	pad thai with chicken (p. 138)

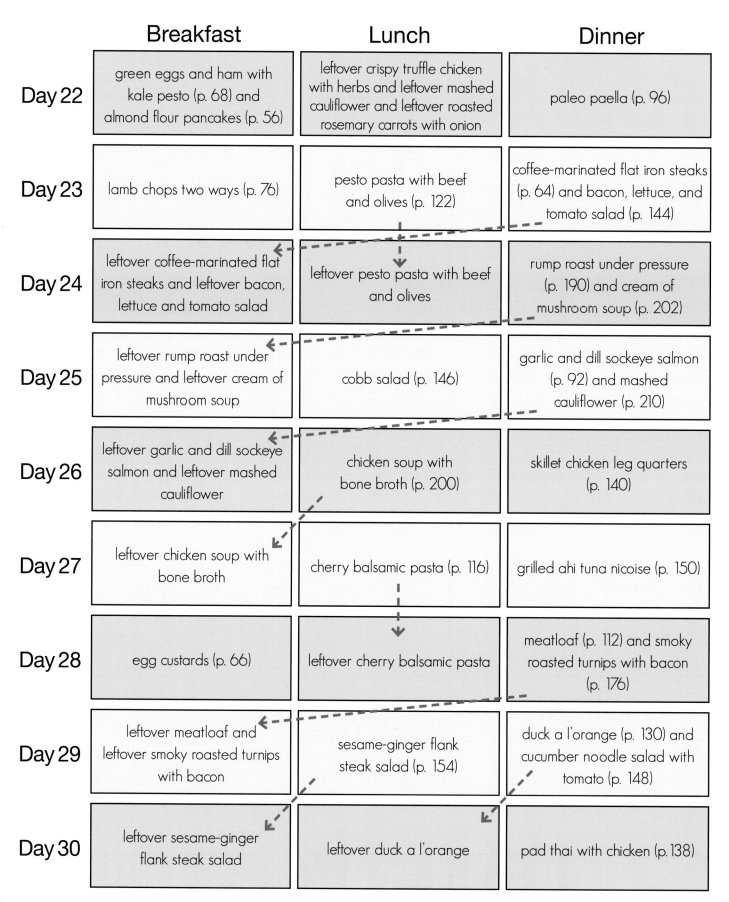

the 30 Day Guide to Paleo Cooking

Week 4
Shopping List

Meat

- [ ] Ahi tuna steak (day 27) - ¾ lb
- [ ] Bacon - 1 lb (save bacon fat for other recipes)
- [ ] Beef bone broth (should be frozen from Week 3) - 2 cups
- [ ] Beef liver - ½ lb
- [ ] Beef rump roast - 3 ½ lbs
- [ ] Chicken bone broth (2 chicken backs and necks) - 4 quarts
- [ ] Chicken breast, boneless skinless - 1 ½ lbs
- [ ] Chicken leg quarters - 2
- [ ] Chicken tenders - ½ lb
- [ ] Chicken thighs, boneless and skinless - 16
- [ ] Duck, whole with skin - 5 lbs
- [ ] Eggs - 18
- [ ] Flank steak - 1 ½ lbs
- [ ] Flat iron steaks - 4
- [ ] Ground beef or lamb - 2 ½ lbs
- [ ] Ground beef - 3 lbs
- [ ] Ham - 6 slices + 1 cup cubed
- [ ] Lamb chops - 6
- [ ] Shrimp (day 22) - ½ lb
- [ ] Sockeye salmon (day 25) - ¾ lb

Vegetables

- [ ] Asparagus - 1 ½ lbs
- [ ] Carrots - 2 lbs
- [ ] Cauliflower - 2 head
- [ ] Celery - 2 heads
- [ ] Cucumbers - 3
- [ ] Green leaf lettuce - 2 heads
- [ ] Iceberg lettuce - ½ cup
- [ ] Kale - 2 cups
- [ ] Red bell peppers - 2
- [ ] Shallots - 2
- [ ] Spaghetti squash - 3 medium
- [ ] Spring mix salad greens - 6 cups
- [ ] Turnips - 4
- [ ] White mushrooms - 3 cups
- [ ] Yellow onions - 8 medium
- [ ] Yellow squash - 4 medium

Fruit

- [ ] Grape tomatoes - 2 cups
- [ ] Kumato (brown tomato) - 1
- [ ] Lemons (for juice) - 2
- [ ] Orange - 1
- [ ] Roma tomato - 1
- [ ] Vine ripe tomato - 1

Fresh Herbs

- [ ] Basil - 1 large bunch (at least 3 packed cups)
- [ ] Chives - 2 Tbsp
- [ ] Cilantro - 1 Tbsp
- [ ] Flat leaf parsley - 1 large bunch
- [ ] Oregano - 1 small bunch
- [ ] Thyme - 3 sprigs

Other

- [ ] Almond butter - ¼ cup
- [ ] Bacon fat - 2 Tbsp
- [ ] Blanched almond flour - 1 ¾ cups
- [ ] Cherry balsamic vinegar - ⅓ cup
- [ ] Coffee, ground - 1 Tbsp
- [ ] Diced tomatoes, no salt added - 1 can (15 oz)
- [ ] Macadamia nuts - ⅓ cup
- [ ] Pine nuts - ⅔ cup
- [ ] Roasted nori sheets
- [ ] Saffron - 4 strands
- [ ] Tomato paste - 1 small can (6 oz)
- [ ] Vanilla
- [ ] Grass-fed butter

Part 3
The Recipes

It's important to educate yourself as to why the Paleo lifestyle is optimal for your body, and the most critical component of the diet is proper nutrition. It's that simple! The foods we eat are where the rubber meets the road.

One of the things we enjoy most about Paleo eating and cooking is that taste is never sacrificed, no matter how simple the meal. Less is more in our minds, especially when cooking with real, whole foods. Oftentimes, all you will need for a quick, easy, mouth-watering meal is a good cooking fat and a little salt and pepper!

As you look through the recipes in this section, you may notice some that are not used in the meal plan. This is completely intentional. We designed the meal plans in this book to accommodate busy schedules, with as many opportunities as possible for easy-to-cook meals, and those that also make extra servings, which can be used as leftovers. The book includes many extra recipes beyond the meal plan for anyone who wishes to change things up, or swap out meals.

Relax, cook, and enjoy.

Reading the Recipe Pages

Type of recipe organized alphabetically and color coded

> ground meat

coffee break sliders

[Serves 4]

Prep Time: 20 minutes
Cook Time: 60 minutes } Total Time: 80 minutes : Difficulty: ⚪ ⚪ ⚪ ⚪ ⚪ : 1 [2] 3 [4]

Recipe name and approximate yield

General recipe information:
- Preparation time
- Cook time
- Total Time
- Degree of difficulty
- Meal planner week(s)

2 Tbsp grass-fed butter

1/4 yellow onion, sliced

1/2 teaspoon salt

1/4 teaspoon ground pepper

1 tablespoon finely ground coffee

1/2 tablespoon salt

1/2 tablespoon adobo seasoning

1 lb grassfed ground beef

6 leaves of green leaf lettuce

1. Heat 2 tablespoons grassfed butter over medium-heat in a heavy skillet.
2. Thinly slice 1/4 onion, and sauté in the skillet until soft.
3. Season onions with salt and pepper, and set aside.
4. Preheat your grill to high-heat (500° F).
5. In a small mixing bowl, combine the ground coffee, salt, and Adobo Seasoning and mix until combined.
6. Form the ground beef into 6 equal portions, and flatten into burgers. Make a slight dimple in the center to keep the burgers from getting too thick in the middle when they cook.
7. Season liberally with the coffee, salt and adobo mixture.
8. Gently place the burgers on the very hot grill, and cook for 4 minutes per side.
9. Serve over fresh green leaf lettuce, topped with the sautéed onions.

Cooking instructions

Ingredient list

breakfast	poultry
chophouse	salads
fish and seafood	side dishes
ground meat	time savers
pasta	soups

Color coding by recipe type

Hayley Mason and Bill Staley

> Let's eat!

almond flour pancakes

[Serves 4]

Prep Time: 10 minutes
Cook Time: 10 minutes } Total Time: 20 minutes

Difficulty: ● ● ○ ○ ○

1 2 3 **4**

2 eggs, whisked

1 3/4 cups blanched almond flour

1/2 teaspoon salt

1/2 teaspoon ground cinnamon

1/4 teaspoon ground nutmeg

1 teaspoon pure vanilla extract

2/3 cup water

1 tablespoon salted grass-fed butter
or coconut oil, for frying

1. In a small mixing bowl, whisk the two eggs.

2. In a medium-sized mixing bowl, combine the almond flour, salt, cinnamon, and nutmeg.

3. Add the vanilla extract and eggs to the dry ingredients. Mix with a wooden spoon to combine.

4. Add water, and stir.

5. Heat 1 tablespoon of grass-fed butter or coconut oil in a large non-stick skillet.

6. Using 1/8 cup, scoop the batter into the frying pan, leaving enough space in between the pancakes to flip.

7. Cook 2 minutes on the first side, flip, and cook for another 1-2 minutes. Add additional cooking fat as needed. (It helps to flip the pancakes back and forth a bit to ensure they are cooked through.)

8. Top with your choice of grass-fed butter or coconut oil and a sprinkle of cinnamon. Serve with any fresh fruit you may have on hand.

breakfast bacon stir-fry

[Serves 2]

Prep Time: 5 minutes
Cook Time: 10 minutes } Total Time: 15 minutes

Difficulty: ⬤ ⭕ ⭕ ⭕ ⭕

| 1 | 2 | 3 | 4 |

4 strips bacon

1 head broccoli, chopped

1 red bell pepper, sliced

1 cup white mushrooms, sliced

2 cups cabbage, shredded

Salt and pepper to taste

1. Heat a heavy skillet over medium-heat.

2. Sauté the bacon until crispy.

3. Add the broccoli, bell pepper, mushrooms, and cabbage.

4. Continue to stir-fry until the vegetables are soft, sprinkling with salt and pepper to taste.

breakfast meatloaf

[Serves 6]

Prep Time: 20 minutes
Cook Time: 35 minutes } Total Time: 55 minutes

Difficulty: ⬤ ⬤ ○ ○ ○   [1] [2] [3] [4]

6 eggs

1 1/2 pounds ground pork

1 teaspoon garlic

1 teaspoon paprika

1/2 teaspoon sage

1 teaspoon fennel seeds

1/4 teaspoon cayenne

1/2 teaspoon salt

1/2 teaspoon black pepper

2 mini-loaf pans

1. Preheat the oven to 400° F.

2. Place the eggs in a saucepan. Cover them with water, and bring to a light boil.

3. Boil the eggs for 10 minutes. Then, place them into an ice water bath, and peel the shells.

4. In a large mixing bowl, combine the pork with the garlic, paprika, sage, fennel seed, cayenne, salt, and black pepper until the mixture reaches an even consistency.

5. Line two mini-loaf pans with small pieces of parchment paper (as shown in the photo).

6. Place a thin layer of the pork mixture in the bottom of the loaf pans. Place the eggs in the loaf pans, and fill in with the remaining pork.

7. Bake the meatloaves for 35 minutes. Slice and serve.

broccoli casserole

[Serves 8]

Prep Time: 20 minutes
Cook Time: 60 minutes } Total Time: 80 minutes Difficulty: ● ● ● ○ ○ | 1 | 2 | **3** | 4 |

1 1/2-2 pounds broccoli florets

1 tablespoon grass-fed butter,

   coconut oil, or duck fat

1 small yellow onion, thinly sliced

2 cloves garlic, minced

16 ounces sliced white mushrooms

1 teaspoon dried thyme

4 eggs, room temperature

1 cup full-fat coconut milk, room

   temperature

Salt and pepper to taste

1. Preheat the oven to 350° F.

2. Boil the broccoli in a large soup pot until fork tender.

3. While the broccoli is boiling, melt the butter in a large skillet over medium-heat.

4. Add the onion to the skillet, and sauté until translucent.

5. Add the garlic and mushrooms to the skillet, season with thyme, salt and pepper, and continue to sauté until tender.

6. While the onion and mushrooms are cooking, drain the water from the broccoli. Allow the broccoli to cool to the touch, and chop any larger pieces into bite-sized pieces.

7. Add the boiled broccoli to the onion and mushrooms, and gently stir until combined.

8. Grease a 9x13-inch baking dish with your choice of cooking fat.

9. Pour the broccoli and mushroom mixture into the well-greased baking dish in an even layer.

10. In a medium-sized mixing bowl, whisk together the eggs and coconut milk.

11. Carefully pour the eggs and coconut milk over the vegetables, being sure to coat all evenly.

12. Season once more with salt and pepper, and place in the oven to bake at 350° F for 1 hour.

coffee-marinated flat iron steaks

[Serves 4]

Prep Time: 4-6 hours
Cook Time: 20 minutes } Total Time: 4-6 hours   Difficulty: ● ● ○ ○ ○   1 2 3 [4]

3/4 cup strongly brewed coffee

1/3 cup coconut aminos

2 cloves garlic, minced

1 shallot, minced

1 teaspoon red pepper flakes

1 teaspoon salt

1 teaspoon black pepper

4 flat Iron steaks

4 eggs

1 tablespoon coconut oil

1. Brew the coffee, and allow it to chill in the refrigerator before making the marinade.

2. In a medium-sized mixing bowl, combine the chilled coffee, coconut aminos, garlic, shallot, red pepper flakes, salt, and black pepper. Whisk to combine.

3. Rinse the steaks under cool water, pat them dry, and place them in a dish.

4. Pour the marinade over the steaks to evenly coat, and refrigerate them in the marinade for at least 4-6 hours, or up to 24 hours.

5. Preheat the grill to medium-high heat.

6. Grill the steaks 12-15 minutes, flipping once.

7. Remove the steaks from the grill, and allow them to rest for 5 minutes.

8. While the steaks are resting, fry the eggs in coconut oil.

9. Top each steak with its own egg, and serve.

egg custards

[Serves 2]

Prep Time: 10 minutes
Cook Time: 35 minutes } Total Time: 45 minutes

Difficulty: ● ● ○ ○ ○

| 1 | 2 | 3 | 4 |

5 strips bacon, cooked and crumbled

1 cup white mushrooms

4 eggs

1/2 cup full-fat coconut milk

Salt and pepper, to taste

2 tablespoons chives, chopped

1. Preheat the oven to 350° F.

2. Fry the bacon in a cast iron skillet on medium-heat until crispy.

3. Remove the bacon from the skillet, and reserve the excess bacon fat in a small glass dish.

4. Sauté the mushrooms in a seasoned skillet until tender (about 3 minutes).

5. In a medium-sized mixing bowl, whisk the eggs and coconut milk until fluffy.

6. Season the eggs with salt and pepper.

7. Crumble the bacon, and add it to the egg mixture.

8. Add the mushrooms and chives, and stir until all are evenly combined.

9. Pour the egg mixture into 4 6-ounce ramekins.

10. Place the ramekins on a baking sheet, and bake for 30-40 minutes or until the eggs are set.

green eggs and ham with kale pesto

[Serves 2]

Prep Time: 25 minutes
Cook Time: 5 minutes } Total Time: 30 minutes   Difficulty: ⚪ ⚪ ⚪ ⚪ ⚪ | 1 | **2** | 3 | **4** |

Kale Pesto

2 cups kale, deveined

1/3 cup pine nuts

1/2 cup olive oil

Juice of 1/2 lemon

Salt and black pepper to taste

Eggs and Ham

1 tablespoon grass-fed butter,
  unsalted

4 eggs

Black pepper to taste

6 pieces ham

Avocado slices for garnish

1. For the pesto, pulse the kale leaves and pine nuts in a food processor.

2. While the mixture is processing, slowly add the olive oil and lemon juice.

3. Add salt and pepper to taste.

4. Continue to process until all ingredients are evenly blended.

5. Heat the butter in a skillet over medium-heat.

6. Crack the eggs into the skillet, sprinkle them with black pepper, and cook on low until the whites are cooked through.

7. In another skillet, fry the ham on medium-heat until crispy.

8. Plate the eggs over the ham, drizzle with the kale pesto, and garnish with avocado slices.

poached eggs with garlicky sprouts

[Serves 2]

Prep Time: 5 minutes
Cook Time: 15 minutes } Total Time: 20 minutes

Difficulty: ● ○ ○ ○ ○

| 1 | 2 | 3 | 4 |

1 tablespoon grass-fed butter or ghee

2 cups Brussels sprouts, sliced

2 teaspoons garlic powder

1/2 teaspoon salt

1 teaspoon black pepper

4 eggs

Black sea salt to garnish (optional)

1. In a skillet over medium-heat, warm the butter.

2. Add the Brussels sprouts to the skillet, and sauté.

3. Sprinkle the Brussels sprouts with the garlic powder, salt, and black pepper. Continue to sauté until the sprouts are tender.

4. Heat some water in an egg poacher. Crack the eggs into the poaching cups, cover with a lid, and cook for 4 minutes.

5. Plate the Brussels sprouts, top them with the poached eggs, and sprinkle with black sea salt.

Note: If you do not have an egg poacher, you can steam the eggs in a skillet, adding 1/4 cup of water, and covering with a lid.

superfood sausages

[Serves 4]

Prep Time: 15 minutes
Cook Time: 8 minutes } Total Time: 23 minutes

Difficulty: ● ● ○ ○ ○   1 2 3 4

1/2 pound beef liver

1 pound ground pork

1/2 small yellow onion, finely diced

Sausage Seasoning (page 212)

1 tablespoon duck fat for frying

1. Grind the beef liver in a food processor.

2. Mix the liver thoroughly with the ground pork.

3. Add the diced onion and Sausage Seasoning, and form the meat into patties.

4. Heat 1 tablespoon of duck fat in a heavy skillet over medium-heat.

5. Cook the patties until they are no longer pink in the center (about 3-4 minutes per side).

beef tenderloin with truffle butter

[Serves 4]

Prep Time: 20 minutes
Cook Time: 2-4 hours } Total Time: 2-4 hours   Difficulty: ● ● ○ ○ ○   1 2 3 4

Compound Herb Butter

1/4 cup grass-fed butter, salted

1/4 cup fresh marjoram, minced

1/4 cup fresh sage, minced

1/2 teaspoon salt

1/2 teaspoon black pepper

4 tenderloin steaks (8 ounces each)

Truffle Butter

1/2 cup grass-fed butter, unsalted

1/2 teaspoon black truffle salt

1. Fill your Sous Vide* with water to within one inch of the max fill line, and set the temperature to 134° F.

2. While the water is heating, make the Compound Herb Butter. Soften 1/4 cup salted grass-fed butter, and mix with the marjoram, sage, salt and pepper.

3. Seal two BPA-free Sous Vide pouches, and line the insides with the Compound Herb Butter.

4. Place two steaks in each pouch, and vacuum seal them. Place them in the water (if it is up to temperature), and set the time for 2-4 hours.

5. To make the Truffle Butter, whip 1/2 cup unsalted grass-fed butter with the 1/2 teaspoon black truffle salt.

6. Preheat your grill to high-heat (about 500° F).

7. Remove the steaks from their pouches, and sear them for 2-3 minutes per side.

8. Serve the tenderloin sliced thinly, topped with the black truffle butter and with a side of Mashed Cauliflower (page 210).

* No Sous vide? No problem! Rub your steaks with the Compound Herb Butter, and cook them on a hot grill. Use a meat thermometer to determine when they have reached an internal temperature of 130° F. Upon removing them from the grill, allow them to rest until their internal temperature reaches 134° F.

lamb chops two ways

[Serves 2]

Prep Time: 10 minutes
Cook Time: 8 minutes } Total Time: 18 minutes   Difficulty: ● ● ○ ○ ○ | 1 | 2 | 3 | **4** |

6 lamb chops

Adobo Seasoning (top in photo)

  6 tablespoons salt

  6 tablespoons granulated garlic

  4 tablespoons oregano

  2 tablespoons black pepper

  2 tablespoons onion powder

Sausage Seasoning (bottom in photo)

  1 teaspoon garlic powder

  1 teaspoon paprika

  1/2 teaspoon rubbed sage

  1 teaspoon fennel seeds

  1/4 teaspoon cayenne powder

  1/4 teaspoon white pepper

  1/2 teaspoon salt

  1/2 teaspoon black pepper

1. Preheat a grill (or grill pan) to high-heat.

2. To make the Adobo Seasoning, blend the salt, granulated garlic, oregano, black pepper and onion powder.

3. To make the Sausage Seasoning, blend the garlic powder, paprika, rubbed sage, fennel seeds, cayenne powder, white pepper, salt, and black pepper.

4. Season the lamb chops liberally with the seasoning blends.

5. Cook the lamb chops over high-heat on the grill or grill pan for 4 minutes per side (or longer, if desired).

6. Allow to rest for 5 minutes, and serve.

sesame beef stir-fry

[Serves 4]

Prep Time: 15 minutes
Cook Time: 45 minutes } Total Time: 1 hour   Difficulty: ○ ○ ○ ○ ○ | 1 | **2** | 3 | 4 |

2 tablespoons duck fat

2 pounds grass-fed beef, cut into
  bite-sized pieces

2 carrots, chopped

3 celery stalks, chopped

1 red bell pepper, sliced

3 cups green cabbage, shredded
  or thinly sliced

2 cups shitake mushroom caps,
  sliced

1/2 cup water chestnuts

2 sprigs green onion, sliced

2 teaspoons garlic powder

2 teaspoons onion powder

1/2 teaspoon ground ginger

1 teaspoon red pepper flakes

1/2 cup coconut aminos

3-5 drops fish sauce

1 tablespoon toasted sesame oil
  (optional, after cooking)

Sesame seeds for garnish

1. In a large enameled pot or cast iron skillet, warm the duck fat.

2. Sear the beef on all sides over high-heat. Remove the beef from the pan and set aside.

3. Reduce the heat to medium, and add the carrots, celery, and red bell pepper. Sauté for 5 minutes or until vegetables begin to soften.

4. Add the cabbage, and continue to sauté, tossing frequently.

5. Once the cabbage has softened, add the mushrooms, water chestnuts, and green onion.

6. Sprinkle with the garlic powder, onion powder, ground ginger, and red pepper flakes, tossing to evenly distribute the spices.

7. When the mushrooms have softened, add the coconut aminos and fish sauce, and sauté for 2 minutes.

8. Add the beef back to the stir-fry, and toss to combine with the vegetables and sauce.

9. Remove from heat, toss with the toasted sesame oil if desired, and serve with a garnish of sesame seeds.

smoky country ribs

[Serves 4]

Prep Time: 10 minutes
Cook Time: 15 minutes } Total Time: 25 minutes | Difficulty: ● ● ○ ○ ○ | 1 2 3 4

2 teaspoons salt

2 teaspoons black pepper

1 tablespoon smoked paprika

1 tablespoon garlic powder

1 tablespoon onion powder

1 tablespoon coriander

1 pound pork country style ribs

Salt and pepper to taste

1. Preheat the grill to medium-heat.

2. Combine the salt, black pepper, smoked paprika, garlic powder, onion powder, and coriander in a small pinch bowl.

3. Rinse the ribs under cold water, and pat dry.

4. Sprinkle the ribs with salt and pepper on both sides.

5. Sprinkle all sides of ribs with the spice blend, and press the spices into the ribs.

6. Grill the ribs over medium-heat for 12-15 minutes or until cooked to desired internal temperature (145-160° F).

spicy cinnamon lamb steaks

[Serves 2]

Prep Time: 10 minutes
Cook Time: 8 minutes } Total Time: 18 minutes   Difficulty: ● ● ○ ○ ○   [1] [2] [3] [4]

1/2 teaspoon garlic powder

1/2 teaspoon coriander

1/2 teaspoon cumin

1/2 teaspoon ground cinnamon

2 lamb steaks (8 ounces each)

1/4 teaspoon red pepper flakes

Salt to taste

1. Preheat the grill to high-heat.

2. In a small mixing bowl, combine the garlic powder, coriander, cumin, and cinnamon.

3. Sprinkle the spice mixture over both sides of the steaks.

4. Add the red pepper flakes to each steak, adding or subtracting quantity depending on your preference for piquance.

5. Sprinkle the steaks with salt to taste on both sides.

6. Grill the steaks for 4 minutes per side (for medium steaks).

7. Allow the steaks to rest for 5 minutes, and serve.

teriyaki baby back ribs

[Serves 6]

Prep Time: 1 hour
Cook Time: 30 minutes } Total Time: 90 minutes : Difficulty: ⬤ ⬤ ⬤ ⬤ ◯ : 1 2 **3** 4

3 pounds pork baby back ribs

Teriyaki Marinade

   1/2 cup coconut aminos

   1/4 cup spicy brown mustard

   3 cloves garlic, minced

   1 teaspoon salt

   1 teaspoon paprika

1. Cut the ribs into 4-5-bone portions. If possible, remove the silver skin from the underside of the ribs.

2. Bring a large pot of water to boil, and parboil the ribs in the water for 30 minutes.

3. While the ribs are cooking, make the marinade. In a small mixing bowl, whisk together the coconut aminos, brown mustard, garlic, salt, and paprika.

4. Remove the ribs from the water, and allow the ribs to cool for 5-10 minutes.

5. Preheat the grill to medium-heat. If using a smoker or wood-fired grill, preheat. The wood fire will need to burn for 15 minutes before it can be used for cooking.

6. Brush the ribs with the marinade, and place the ribs meat side down on the hot grill. Allow the ribs to sear for a few minutes.

7. Flip the ribs, and move them to a cooler part of the grill. If using a smoker or wood-fired grill, smoke the ribs for 25 minutes. For most other grills, cook the ribs over low, indirect heat for 20 minutes.

8. Continue to brush the ribs with the marinade, layering the flavor onto the ribs.

9. Allow the ribs to rest for 5 minutes before cutting them into individual portions.

winter savory garlic chops

[Serves 2]

Prep Time: 10 minutes
Cook Time: 10 minutes } Total Time: 20 minutes

Difficulty: ● ○ ○ ○ ○

| 1 | 2 | 3 | 4 |

4 chops (lamb, goat, or pork)

Salt and pepper to taste

4 cloves garlic, minced

5 sprigs fresh savory, minced

1. Rinse the chops under cool water, and pat dry with a paper towel.

2. Sprinkle each side with salt and pepper.

3. Lightly press the garlic and savory into the meat. Flip the meal over, and repeat.

4. Grill the chops on medium-high heat 4-5 minutes per side.

bacon wrapped mahi-mahi

[Serves 4]

Prep Time: 5 minutes
Cook Time: 25 minutes } Total Time: 30 minutes   Difficulty: ⬤ ⬤ ⬤ ◯ ◯   1 2 3 4

1 1/2 pounds Mahi-Mahi

BBQ Blend Spice Mix (page 212)

4 strips bacon

Salt and pepper to taste

1. Preheat the oven to 425° F.

2. Rinse the Mahi-Mahi under cold water, and pat dry.

3. Cut the Mahi-Mahi into four equal portions.

4. Season each filet with the BBQ Blend Spice Mix.

5. Wrap each filet with a strip of bacon, and top with additional salt and pepper to taste.

6. Bake the filets in a baking dish for 25-30 minutes until the fish easily flakes.

creole yellow tail snapper

[Serves 2]

Prep Time: 10 minutes
Cook Time: 30 minutes } Total Time: 40 minutes   Difficulty: ⦿ ⦿ ⦿ ○ ○ | 1 | 2 | 3 | 4 |

1 yellow tail snapper

4 cloves garlic, smashed

2 tablespoons Creole Seasoning
   (page 212)

1/2 lemon

1 rosemary stalk

2 tablespoons grass-fed butter,
   unsalted

1. Preheat the oven to 425° F.

2. Rinse the snapper, and pat dry.

3. Rub the smashed garlic all over the skin of the fish. Then, place the garlic inside the fish body cavity.

4. Season the body cavity with the Creole Seasoning.

5. Rub the lemon on the skin of the fish, and also place it in the body cavity, along with the rosemary.

6. Season the skin of the fish liberally with the remaining Creole Seasoning.

7. Bake the snapper on a roasting rack or broiler pan for 30 minutes until the fish easily flakes.

8. Melt the butter, brush it over the cooked fish, and serve.

garlic and dill sockeye salmon

[Serves 4]

Prep Time: 10 minutes
Cook Time: 30 minutes } Total Time: 40 minutes : Difficulty: ⬤ ⬤ ⬤ ○ ○ : 1 2 3 4

3 tablespoons grass-fed butter, unsalted and divided

3/4 pound sockeye salmon

1/2 teaspoon salt

1/2 teaspoon black pepper

1 teaspoon garlic powder

1 teaspoon dried dill

3 cloves garlic, minced

1. Preheat your oven to 400° F.

2. Place three tablespoons of the butter on the bottom of a large baking dish, divided into several equal portions.

3. Rinse the salmon under cool water, and pat dry.

4. Place the salmon in the large baking dish.

5. Sprinkle the salmon with the salt, black pepper, garlic powder, and dried dill.

6. Place one tablespoon of butter, divided into four equal portions, on top of the salmon.

7. Bake the salmon for 20 minutes.

8. Remove the salmon from the oven, and add the minced garlic to the dish.

9. Bake the salmon for an additional 10 minutes before serving.

lemon butter cod with tartar sauce

[Serves 2]

Prep Time: 15 minutes
Cook Time: 20 minutes } Total Time: 35 minutes

Difficulty: ● ○ ○ ○ ○

| 1 | 2 | 3 | 4 |

Tartar Sauce

2 tablespoons pickles, diced*

1/4 cup mayonnaise (page 168)

1/2 teaspoon dried dill weed

1 teaspoon lemon zest

1/4 teaspoon salt

Cod

1 pound cod filet

1 teaspoon salt

1 teaspoon black pepper

2 tablespoons grass-fed butter,
unsalted

1 lemon, thinly sliced

1/4 cup Tartar Sauce (see above)

* Look for Bubbie's fermented pickles in your local store. Or, if you'd like to make your own, visit our website, www.primalpalate.com, and search for "pickles" in the Recipes section.

1. To make the tartar sauce, combine the diced pickles and mayonnaise in a small mixing bowl.

2. Sprinkle the dill, lemon zest, and salt into the mayonnaise, and stir to combine.

3. Preheat the oven to 425° F.

4. Rinse the cod under cool water, and pat dry with a paper towel.

5. Place the cod into an oven-safe baking dish.

6. Sprinkle the cod with salt and pepper.

7. Lay the butter on top of the cod filets, two pieces per 4 ounces of fish.

8. Lay the lemon slices on top of the cod filets, two slices per 4 ounces of fish.

9. Bake the cod uncovered for 30 minutes, and serve with the Tartar Sauce.

paleo paella

[Serves 2]

Prep Time: 10 minutes
Cook Time: 30 minutes } Total Time: 40 minutes   Difficulty: ◉ ◉ ◉ ○ ○   [1] **2** [3] **4**

1 head cauliflower, grated

1 tablespoon ghee

1 large carrot, peeled and diced

1 red bell pepper, diced

1 small yellow onion, diced

3 garlic cloves, smashed

1/2 pound boneless, skinless
chicken breasts, cut into bite-
sized pieces

1/2 pound wild-caught shrimp,
peeled and deveined

4 strands saffron

1 teaspoon turmeric

2 teaspoons smoked paprika

1/4 teaspoon chipotle powder

Salt and pepper to taste

1 handful flat leaf parsley plus
extra for garnish

1. Using a box grater or food processor, shred the cauliflower florets into a rice-like texture.

2. In a large Dutch oven, heat the ghee over medium-heat.

3. Add the carrot, red bell pepper, and onion to the Dutch oven, and sauté until the veggies have softened.

4. Add the smashed garlic cloves to the Dutch oven along with the chicken breasts. Continue to sauté for 2 minutes.

5. Add the shrimp to the Dutch oven, and sauté until the shrimp is no longer translucent.

6. Season with the saffron, turmeric, smoked paprika, and chipotle powder, stirring to make sure the seasonings are evenly distributed.

7. Add the riced cauliflower to the pot, and stir to combine.

8. Season with salt and pepper, and add the parsley. Continue to cook while stirring until the cauliflower has softened.

9. Garnish with extra parsley if desired, and serve.

sesame tuna wraps

[Serves 2]

Prep Time: 15 minutes
Cook Time: 4-6 minutes } Total Time: 20 minutes   Difficulty: ● ● ● ○ ○   1 2 3 4

1 tablespoon coconut oil

3/4 pound yellowtail tuna

Salt and pepper to taste

Sesame-Ginger Sauce

    1/2 cup coconut aminos

    1/4 cup toasted sesame oil

    1/4 teaspoon red pepper

      flakes

    1/2 teaspoon ground ginger

4 roasted Nori sheets

1/2 avocado

1/2 cup cucumber, sliced

1/2 cup iceberg lettuce, shredded

1. Heat the coconut oil in a heavy skillet over medium-high heat.

2. Season the tuna on both sides with salt and pepper.

3. Sear the tuna for 2-3 minutes per side.

4. Remove the tuna from the skillet, and allow it to rest for 2 minutes before slicing.

5. In a mixing bowl, make the Sesame-Ginger Sauce by whisking together the coconut aminos, toasted sesame oil, red pepper flakes, and ground ginger. Set aside.

6. Place a small amount of the sliced tuna down the center of a Nori sheet, and top with the avocado, sliced cucumber, and shredded lettuce.

7. Drizzle with the Sesame-Ginger Sauce, roll up, and serve.

tandoori shrimp stir-fry

[Serves 4]

Prep Time: 15 minutes
Cook Time: 15 minutes } Total Time: 30 minutes   Difficulty: ⬤ ⬤ ○ ○ ○   [1] [2] [3] [4]

1 1/2 pound wild-caught shrimp, peeled and deveined

1 tablespoon ghee

1 small yellow onion, diced

1 red bell pepper, diced

2 teaspoons garlic powder

1/2 teaspoon salt

1/2 teaspoon black pepper

1 tablespoon Tandoori spice blend

1/2 teaspoon red pepper flakes

1 tablespoon coconut aminos

Shredded lettuce

1. Rinse the shrimp under cool water, and pat dry.

2. In a large skillet, melt the ghee over medium-heat.

3. Add the onion and red bell pepper, and sauté until the onion is translucent.

4. Add the shrimp to the skillet, and continue to sauté until the shrimp is pink and no longer translucent.

5. Season with garlic powder, salt, pepper, Tandoori spice blend, red pepper flakes, and coconut aminos. Stir until the shrimp is evenly seasoned.

6. Serve over shredded lettuce.

beef and mushroom lettuce wraps

[Serves 4]

Prep Time: 10 minutes
Cook Time: 25 minutes } Total Time: 35 minutes

Difficulty: ●　●　●　○　○

| 1 | 2 | 3 | 4 |

2 pounds ground beef

1 cup white mushrooms, sliced

1/2 yellow onion, sliced

4 cloves garlic, minced

4 tablespoons BBQ Blend Spice

   Mix (page 212)

1 tablespoon salt

1 tablespoon pepper

1/2 avocado

1/4 cup cilantro

1 head iceberg lettuce

1. Brown the beef in a large Dutch oven over medium-heat.

2. Once the beef is cooked, toss in the mushrooms, onion, and minced garlic.

3. Top with the BBQ Blend Spice Mix and salt and pepper, and cook, stirring often for 20 minutes.

4. Place the meat into individual lettuce cups, top with avocado and cilantro, and serve.

coffee break sliders

[Serves 4]

Prep Time: 20 minutes
Cook Time: 8 minutes
} Total Time: 28 minutes : Difficulty: ○ ● ○ ○ ○ : 1 **2** 3 4

2 tablespoons grass-fed butter, unsalted

1/4 yellow onion, sliced

1/2 teaspoon salt

1/4 teaspoon ground pepper

1 tablespoon finely ground coffee

1/2 tablespoon salt

1/2 tablespoon Adobo Seasoning (page 212)

1 pound grass-fed ground beef

6 leaves of green leaf lettuce

1. In a heavy skillet, heat the grass-fed butter over medium-heat.

2. Add the sliced onion, and sauté in the skillet until soft.

3. Season the onion with salt and pepper, and set aside.

4. Preheat the grill to high-heat (500° F).

5. In a small mixing bowl, combine the ground coffee, salt, and Adobo Seasoning, and mix until combined.

6. Form the ground beef into 6 equal portions, and flatten into burgers. Make a slight dimple in the center of each patty to keep the burgers from getting too thick in the middle when they cook.

7. Season the meat liberally with the coffee, salt, and Adobo mixture.

8. Gently place the burgers on the very hot grill, and cook for 4 minutes per side.

9. Serve the burgers over fresh green leaf lettuce, topped with the sautéed onions.

fajita lettuce wraps with chipotle aioli

[Serves 2]

Prep Time: 15 minutes
Cook Time: 20 minutes } Total Time: 35 minutes

Difficulty: ⭘ ⭘ ⭘ ⭘ ⭘

| 1 | **2** | 3 | 4 |

1/2 tablespoon chipotle powder

1 tablespoon smoked paprika

1 tablespoon onion powder

1 tablespoon garlic powder

1 teaspoon salt

2 teaspoons black pepper

2 tablespoons ghee

1 red bell pepper, sliced

1 cup white mushrooms, sliced

1 small yellow onion, thinly sliced

1/2 pound flank steak, thinly sliced

Chipotle Aioli

    Mayonnaise (page 168)

     1 teaspoon chipotle powder

1 head Iceberg lettuce

1 avocado

1. In a small mixing bowl, combine 1/2 tablespoon chipotle powder, the smoked paprika, onion powder, garlic powder, salt, and black pepper. Set aside.

2. Melt 1 tablespoon of ghee in a large skillet over medium-high heat.

3. Add the red bell pepper, mushrooms, and onions to the skillet and sauté, seasoning liberally with the spice mixture.

4. When the onions and peppers are soft, transfer the vegetables to a bowl, and set aside.

5. Season the steak with the spice blend. Add the remaining tablespoon of ghee to the skillet. Next, add the steak to the hot skillet, and cook 4-6 minutes.

6. Season the mayonnaise with 1 teaspoon of chipotle powder, and whisk to combine.

7. Place the steak and vegetables in a lettuce cup, and top with avocado and Chipotle Aioli to serve.

ground pork in endive boats

[Serves 4]

Prep Time: 15 minutes
Cook Time: 10 minutes } Total Time: 25 minutes

Difficulty: ⦿ ⦿ ⦿ ○ ○

| 1 | 2 | 3 | 4 |

1 pound ground pork

5 cloves garlic, minced

2 teaspoons ginger root, minced

2 tablespoons chives, chopped

1/4 teaspoon red pepper flakes

1/4 teaspoon fish sauce

1 teaspoon black pepper

1 head Belgian endive

1 radish, thinly sliced for garnish

1. Heat a cast iron skillet on medium-heat.

2. Place the ground pork in the skillet, and crumble it using a high-heat rubber scraper.

3. Add the garlic, ginger, chives, and red pepper flakes to the meat, and continue to brown.

4. When the meat is almost cooked completely, add the fish sauce and black pepper.

5. Stir the meat constantly to ensure that the fish sauce is evenly distributed.

6. Remove the pork from the heat, and cool.

7. Serve in endive boats, and garnish with slivers of radish.

lamb asparagus stir-fry

[Serves 4]

Prep Time: 15 minutes
Cook Time: 45 minutes } Total Time: 1 hour   Difficulty: ⬤ ⬤ ⬤ ◯ ◯   1 | 2 | 3 | 4

1 pound ground lamb or beef

2 tablespoons duck fat, divided

2 teaspoon salt, divided

1 clove garlic, pressed

1 teaspoon ginger, minced

1 teaspoon garlic powder

1 teaspoon red pepper flakes

1/2 large yellow onion, thinly sliced

2 cups shitake mushrooms, sliced

1 pound asparagus, cut into 1-inch
   pieces

1 medium cabbage, thinly sliced

1 tablespoon sesame seeds

2 tablespoons coconut aminos

2 tablespoons toasted sesame oil

1. Brown the ground meat in 1 tablespoon of duck fat with 1 teaspoon of salt, as well as the garlic, ginger, garlic powder, and red pepper flakes.

2. Add the onions, mushrooms, and asparagus, and toss.

3. In a separate pan, sauté the cabbage over medium-heat in 1 tablespoon of duck fat, turning occasionally to cook evenly.

4. Sprinkle with 1 teaspoon salt.

5. Sprinkle the ground meat and veggies with the sesame seeds, toss, reduce heat to low, and add the coconut aminos and sesame oil.

6. When the cabbage noodles are soft, remove them from the heat, plate, and top with the meat and vegetables.

meatloaf

[Serves 8]

Prep Time: 20 minutes
Cook Time: 60 minutes } Total Time: 80 minutes

Difficulty: ⦿ ⦿ ⦿ ○ ○

1　2　3　**4**

2 1/2 pounds ground beef or
　lamb

1/2 pound beef liver

3 medium-sized carrots, peeled
　and chopped

2 celery stalks, chopped

1 small yellow onion, chopped

1 teaspoon salt

2 teaspoons black pepper

1 tablespoon onion powder

1 tablespoon garlic powder

2 tablespoons coconut aminos

1 egg, whisked

Sauce

　7 ounces tomato paste

　1/4 cup coconut aminos

　1/2 teaspoon salt

　1/2 teaspoon black pepper

　2 teaspoons hot sauce
　(preferably Frank's)

1. Preheat the oven to 375° F.

2. Place the ground meat in a large mixing bowl.

3. Place the beef liver, carrots, celery, and onion into a food processor, and pulse until minced.

4. Add the minced liver and vegetables to the mixing bowl with the ground meat.

5. Season the mixture with salt, pepper, onion powder, garlic powder, and coconut aminos.

6. Add the egg, and mix all ingredients until evenly combined.

7. Pack the meatloaf mixture into a loaf pan.

8. Line a baking sheet with parchment paper, and carefully place the loaf pan, open side down, onto the baking sheet.

9. Carefully remove the loaf pan from the meatloaf.

10. Bake the meatloaf for 1 hour or until it reaches 170° F internally.

11. To make the sauce, combine the tomato paste, coconut aminos, salt, pepper, and hot sauce in a small saucepan, and heat over medium-heat.

12. Bring to a boil while stirring. Reduce to low-heat, and simmer the sauce for 20 minutes.

13. Slice the meatloaf, top with the sauce, and serve.

shepherd's pie

[Serves 8]

Prep Time: 20 minutes
Cook Time: 55 minutes } Total Time: 75 minutes : Difficulty: ● ● ○ ○ ○ : 1 2 3 4

1 tablespoon grass-fed butter, unsalted

1 yellow onion, thinly sliced

2 large carrots, grated

1 zucchini, grated

1 yellow squash, grated

Salt and pepper to taste

2 heads cauliflower

2 pounds ground beef, pork, or lamb

2 tablespoons Sausage Seasoning (page 212)

1. Preheat the oven to 350° F.

2. Melt the butter in a heavy skillet over medium-heat.

3. Sauté the onion, carrots, zucchini, and yellow squash until tender, and season with salt and pepper to taste.

4. Chop the cauliflower into small chunks, and cover it with water in a large soup pot.

5. Bring the water to a boil, cover it with a lid, and cook the cauliflower until fork tender (about 15 minutes).

6. Season the ground meat with the Sausage Seasoning, and mix thoroughly.

7. Place the meat in a 9x13-inch baking dish, and pat it down to a uniform thickness.

8. Cover the meat with an even layer of the sautéed vegetables, and bake for 40 minutes.

9. Drain the water from the cauliflower, and place the cauliflower in a food processor or high speed blender, processing until creamy.

10. Remove the meat from the oven, and set the oven to broil on high.

11. Pour an even layer of the cauliflower over the meat, and broil for 10-15 minutes until the cauliflower has golden peaks.

cherry balsamic pasta

[Serves 4]

Prep Time: 15 minutes
Cook Time: 45 minutes } Total Time: 1 hour

Difficulty: ● ● ● ○ ○

1 2 3 **4**

1 spaghetti squash

1 teaspoon coconut oil

3 cloves garlic, minced

1 yellow onion, diced

1 pound ground beef

1/3 cup cherry balsamic vinegar

1 can diced tomatoes, no salt added (15 ounces)

1 tomato, diced

2 teaspoons salt

1 teaspoon black pepper

1 sprig fresh basil, minced

1 sprig fresh oregano, minced

1. Preheat the oven to 400° F.

2. Remove the stem from the spaghetti squash with a sharp knife, and cut the squash in half, lengthwise.

3. Scoop out the seeds, and place the squash on a baking sheet.

4. Bake for 45 minutes.

5. Meanwhile, heat a large soup pot on medium-heat.

6. Add 1 teaspoon of coconut oil to the pot, followed by the garlic and onion.

7. Add the ground meat, and stir constantly, breaking up the chunks of meat and making sure the garlic and onion do not burn.

8. Once the meat is browned and the onion and garlic are translucent, add the cherry balsamic vinegar, and continue to stir.

9. Add the diced tomatoes, salt, and pepper, and continue to stir until evenly combined.

10. Add the basil and oregano, and stir to combine.

11. Turn the heat down to low, cover, and simmer until the spaghetti squash is done.

12. Once the squash has cooled a bit, scoop out the inside with a fork, and plate the dish.

meatballs with artichoke hearts

[Serves 4]

Prep Time: 15 minutes
Cook Time: 60 minutes } Total Time: 75 minutes

Difficulty: ● ● ● ○ ○

| 1 | 2 | 3 | 4 |

1 spaghetti squash

2 tablespoons Sausage Seasoning (page 212)

2 pounds ground pork

2 tablespoons grass-fed butter, unsalted

2 cups artichoke hearts

2 cups white mushrooms, sliced

2 cloves garlic, minced

Salt and pepper

1/4 cup fresh basil

1. Preheat the oven to 350° F.

2. Slice the spaghetti squash in half, lengthwise, and scoop out the seeds.

3. Place the halves in a baking dish, and bake for 45 minutes until fork tender.

4. Mix the ground pork with the Sausage Seasoning.

5. Roll the pork into 1-2-ounce meatballs, and place them in a separate baking dish.

6. Bake the meatballs for 25 minutes.

7. Meanwhile, heat the butter in a heavy skillet over medium-heat.

8. Sauté the artichoke hearts, mushrooms, and garlic with the salt and pepper until soft.

9. Add the basil, and continue to sauté for 1-2 minutes.

10. Remove the spaghetti squash from the oven, and shred it with a fork. You can add additional butter and seasonings to the spaghetti squash, if desired.

11. Toss the vegetables with the meatballs, and serve over the spaghetti squash.

pasta with meatballs

[Serves 4]

Prep Time: 20 minutes
Cook Time: 45 minutes } Total Time: 1 hour

Difficulty: ● ● ● ○ ○

1 2 **3** 4

1 spaghetti squash

Meatballs

   2 pounds ground pork

   3 tablespoons Adobo

   Seasoning (page 212)

   1 tablespoon salt

   1 teaspoon black pepper

Sauce

   1 tablespoon duck fat

   2 cloves garlic, minced

   1/4 cup onion, diced

   2 cups sliced white

   mushrooms

   2 teaspoons dried basil

   2 teaspoons dried oregano

   6 ounces tomato paste

   2 cups strained tomatoes

   1/4 cup black olives

   2 tablespoons capers

   Salt and pepper to taste

1. Preheat the oven to 400° F.

2. Cut the ends off of the squash, and slice it in half, lengthwise. Scoop out the seeds from the squash, place it on a rimmed baking sheet, and bake for 35 minutes or until squash is tender and the "noodles" shred easily with a fork.

3. In a large mixing bowl, season the ground pork with the Adobo Seasoning, salt, and black pepper.

4. Form the meat mixture into 1-ounce meatballs, and place them in a baking dish.

5. After 35 minutes, remove the squash from the oven, and allow it to cool. Turn the oven down to 350° F.

6. Bake the meatballs at 350° F for 25-30 minutes.

7. While the meatballs and squash are baking, begin to make the sauce. Add the duck fat to a heavy sauce pan, and heat it over medium-heat.

8. Add the garlic and onion to the saucepan, and sauté until the onion is translucent.

9. Add the mushrooms to the saucepan, season with dried basil and dried oregano, and sauté until the mushrooms start to soften.

10. Add the tomato paste, strained tomatoes, black olives, and capers, and stir to combine all ingredients evenly.

11. Season the mixture with salt and pepper to taste, bring to a boil, reduce to a simmer, cover, and allow it to simmer until the dish is ready to be plated.

12. In a large mixing bowl, toss the spaghetti squash "noodles" with the sauce and meatballs. Plate and serve.

pesto pasta with beef and olives

[Serves 6]

Prep Time: 15 minutes
Cook Time: 35 minutes } Total Time: 50 minutes   Difficulty: ⬤ ⬤ ⬤ ○ ○   1 2 3 4

2 large spaghetti squash

Basil Pesto

   2 cups fresh basil, packed

   1 clove garlic, smashed

   1/3 cup pine nuts

   1/2 cup lemon juice

   1/2 cup olive oil

   1/2 teaspoon salt

2 tablespoons grass-fed butter, salted

1/2 yellow onion, diced

2 pounds ground beef

Salt and pepper to taste

1 teaspoon garlic powder

1 cup Kalamata olives

1. Preheat the oven to 425° F.

2. Cut the spaghetti squash in half, lengthwise, and scoop out the seeds.

3. Place the spaghetti squash halves in a baking dish, and bake for 35 minutes.

4. In a food processor, make the pesto by pulsing the basil, garlic, and pine nuts together.

5. Add the lemon juice, olive oil, and salt to the food processor, and blend until smooth. Set the pesto aside.

6. Heat the butter in a large skillet over medium-heat.

7. Add the diced onion, and sauté until the onion is soft.

8. Add the ground beef to the skillet, and season with salt, pepper, and garlic powder.

9. Continue to sauté until the beef has fully cooked. Set aside.

10. Once the spaghetti squash has fully baked, remove it from the oven, and shred it with a fork.

11. Toss the squash noodles with the pesto, adding the seasoned ground beef and olives.

baked chicken thigh wraps

[Serves 4]

Prep Time: 15 minutes
Cook Time: 45 minutes } Total Time: 1 hour

Difficulty: ● ● ● ● ○   1 **2** 3 4

8 chicken thighs, bone in and skin on

2 teaspoons salt

2 teaspoons black pepper

2 teaspoons garlic powder

2 teaspoons onion powder

1 head iceberg lettuce

2 vine-ripened tomatoes

1 avocado

Spicy brown mustard and mayonnaise (page 168) for topping, optional

1. Preheat the oven to 425° F.

2. Rinse the chicken under cool water, and pat dry with a paper towel.

3. Place the chicken on a baking sheet, and set aside.

4. Meanwhile, in a small mixing bowl, combine the salt, black pepper, garlic powder, and onion powder.

5. Sprinkle each chicken thigh liberally with the seasoning mixture.

6. Bake the chicken thighs for 45 minutes.

7. When done, remove the chicken thighs from the oven, and cool them to the touch.

8. Peel the lettuce leaves off of the head, and wash them under cool water. Pat them dry with a paper towel, or dry them in a salad spinner.

9. Rinse and slice the tomato.

10. Peel, pit, and slice the avocado.

11. To plate the dish, tear pieces of the chicken off of the bone, and stuff each lettuce leaf with chicken, tomato, and avocado.

12. Top with spicy mustard and mayonnaise, if desired.

butterflied roast chicken

[Serves 4]

Prep Time: 10 minutes
Cook Time: 1 hours } Total Time: 70 minutes   Difficulty: ● ● ○ ○ ○ | 1 | 2 | 3 | 4 |

1 whole chicken, butterflied

2 tablespoons duck fat

4 cloves garlic, minced

1 tablespoon fresh thyme, minced

1 teaspoon salt

1 teaspoon pepper

1. Rinse the chicken under cool water, and pat dry.

2. Place the chicken on a cutting board, breast side down, and remove the backbone with kitchen scissors or a sharp knife. Freeze the backbone for future stock, if desired.

3. Turn the chicken over, and press down on it until the bones crack slightly and the chicken lays flat.

4. Melt 2 tablespoons of duck fat, and stir in the minced garlic and thyme.

5. Sprinkle in the salt and pepper, and stir to combine.

6. Carefully lift the skin of the chicken to create a space to stuff the duck fat and herbs.

7. Rub the duck fat mixture all over the chicken under the skin, being sure to cover as much of the breasts and legs as possible.

8. Flip the chicken over, and rub the duck fat over the bone side. Sprinkle with salt and pepper.

9. Flipping the chicken back over, rub the breast side entirely with duck fat, and sprinkle with salt and pepper.

10. Place the chicken on a baking sheet, breast side up, and bake at 500° F for 30 minutes.

11. After 30 minutes, turn the heat down to 450° F, and bake for an additional 20-30 minutes before serving.

crispy truffle chicken with herbs

[Serves 4]

Prep Time: 20 minutes
Cook Time: 25 minutes per pound
} Total Time: 2 hours, 50 minutes

Difficulty: ● ● ○ ○ ○

| 1 | 2 | **3** | 4 |

6 pound chicken

3 tablespoons duck fat, melted

1 tablespoon Poultry Blend Spices

   2 tablespoon dried rosemary

   1 tablespoon dried sage

   1 tablespoon dried thyme

   1 teaspoon salt

   1 teaspoon black pepper

   1/4 teaspoon lemon zest

2 teaspoons truffle salt

1/2 teaspoon black pepper

1. Preheat the oven to 350° F.

2. Rinse the chicken under cool water, including the body cavity. Pat dry thoroughly, including the body cavity.

3. Mix the duck fat with the Poultry Blend Spices.

4. Massage the duck fat and spices over the entire chicken, including the body cavity.

5. Sprinkle with truffle salt and black pepper.

6. Place the chicken in a roasting pan, and roast for 25 minutes per pound or until it reaches 165° F in the breast.

7. Baste the chicken with pan drippings at least once, about 30 minutes before it finishes cooking.

duck a l'orange

[Serves 4]

Prep Time: 15 minutes
Cook Time: 1 hour, 45 minutes } Total Time: 2 hours : Difficulty: ○ ○ ○ ○ ○ : 1 2 3 **4**

5 carrots, rinsed and cut into chunks

1 head celery, cut into chunks

2 yellow onions, cut into large chunks

5 pounds duck, skin on

2 tablespoons duck fat

2 teaspoons salt

2 teaspoons black pepper

2 teaspoons coriander

2 teaspoons cumin

3 sprigs thyme

3 sprigs parsley

1 orange, quartered, reserve juice from 1/2

1/2 cup Chicken Bone Broth (page 196)

1. Preheat the oven to 475° F, and place the oven rack in the middle position.

2. Place the carrots, celery, and onions in the bottom of a large roasting pan or Dutch oven.

3. Rinse the duck under cool water, being sure to rinse out the body cavity as well. Pat entire duck dry, including the body cavity.

4. Rub the duck with the duck fat, inside and out.

5. Sprinkle salt and pepper over the entire duck, including inside the body cavity.

6. Combine the coriander, cumin, thyme, and parsley, and rub the duck with the herb mixture.

7. Place a few chunks of onion, celery, and carrot inside the duck, leaving room for the herbs and orange.

8. Stuff the duck with the herbs. Cut the orange into quarters, and stuff two quarters into the duck as well.

9. Place the duck over the vegetables in the roasting pan, and roast for 30 minutes.

10. After 30 minutes, pour the Chicken Bone Broth and the juice of remaining half the orange over the vegetables in the bottom of the pan, and turn the oven down to 350° F.

11. Roast the duck until the thermometer reads 170° F in the thigh (about 60-75 minutes longer).

12. Remove the duck from the oven, allow it to rest for 15 minutes, carve, and serve.

garlic ginger chicken

[Serves 4]

Prep Time: 15 minutes
Cook Time: 45 minutes } Total Time: 1 hour

Difficulty: ● ● ● ○ ○

| 1 | 2 | **3** | 4 |

2 tablespoons grass-fed butter, unsalted

1 tablespoon ginger root, minced

5 cloves garlic, smashed and minced

1/4 teaspoon fish sauce

1/4 cup coconut aminos

8 chicken thighs

1 teaspoon salt

1 teaspoon black pepper

1. Preheat the oven to 425° F.

2. In a small saucepan, melt the butter on low-heat.

3. Turn the heat to medium, and add the ginger, garlic, fish sauce, and coconut aminos to the butter.

4. Allow the mixture to come to a bubble, and stir for 1-2 minutes. Remove from heat, and set aside.

5. Place the chicken thighs in an oven-safe baking dish, and pour the sauce over the chicken.

6. Sprinkle each chicken thigh with salt and pepper.

7. Bake the chicken for 45 minutes, and allow it to cool slightly before serving.

baked half-chicken

[Serves 2]

Prep Time: 5 minutes
Cook Time: 45 minutes } Total Time: 50 minutes   Difficulty: ● ● ○ ○ ○   1 2 3 4

1/2 chicken (about 3 pounds)

1 medium yellow onion, sliced

Salt and pepper to taste

1. Preheat the oven to 425° F.

2. Place the sliced onion on the bottom of a roasting pan.

3. Place the half-chicken on top of the onions, and sprinkle with salt and pepper.

4. Bake for 45 minutes until the chicken reads 165° F in the thickest part of the breast.

5. Serve the chicken topped with the cooked onions.

harvest spiced drumsticks

[Serves 4]

Prep Time: 5 minutes
Cook Time: 40 minutes } Total Time: 45 minutes

Difficulty: ● ○ ○ ○ ○

| 1 | 2 | 3 | 4 |

12 chicken drumsticks

2 tablespoons garam masala

1 teaspoon sea salt

1 teaspoon black pepper

1. Preheat the oven to 425° F.

2. Rinse the chicken under cold water, and pat it dry with a paper towel.

3. Place the drumsticks evenly spaced on a parchment-lined baking sheet.

4. Sprinkle each drumstick generously with garam masala, salt, and black pepper.

5. Bake the drumsticks for 35-40 minutes.

6. Remove them from them oven, and cool slightly before serving.

pad thai with chicken

[Serves 2]

Prep Time: 15 minutes
Cook Time: 15 minutes } Total Time: 30 minutes Difficulty: ⚪ ⚪ ⚪ ⚪ ⚪ | 1 | 2 | 3 | **4** |

4 yellow squash, julienned or spiral sliced into "noodles"

2 chicken breasts, skinless and cubed

1/4 cup almond butter

1/2 cup coconut aminos

1/4 teaspoon fish sauce

1 lime, half for juice, remaining half cut into wedges for garnish

1 teaspoon salt

1 tablespoon sesame oil

1 shallot, minced

3 cloves garlic, minced

1 teaspoon red pepper flakes (optional)

1/3 cup raw macadamia nuts chopped (reserve some for garnish)

1/8 cup cilantro, chopped for garnish

1. Peel the yellow squash using a julienne peeler or spiral slicer. Place the squash in a steamer basket, and steam for 5-8 minutes. Remove the "noodles" before they become too soft.

2. Heat a wok to high-heat. While the wok is heating, cut the chicken breasts into small bite-sized cubes.

3. Mix almond butter with coconut aminos, fish sauce, juice of 1/2 lime, and salt.

4. When wok is very hot, add the sesame oil.

5. Add the cubed chicken to the wok, and stir-fry the chicken until it is cooked through to opaque and white.

6. Add the minced shallot, minced garlic, and sprinkle with red pepper flakes. Continue to stir-fry for 1 minute.

7. Add the chopped macadamia nuts, and continue to stir-fry for 2 minutes.

8. Pour in the sauce mixture, and toss until the chicken and other ingredients are evenly coated.

9. Reduce the heat, and gently toss in the yellow squash noodles.

10. Serve the Pad Thai garnished with cilantro, chopped macadamia nuts, and a squeeze of fresh lime juice.

skillet chicken leg quarters

[Serves 2]

Prep Time: 5 minutes
Cook Time: 45 minutes } Total Time: 50 minutes

Difficulty: ● ● ● ○ ○

| 1 | 2 | 3 | 4 |

3 tablespoons grass-fed butter, salted

2 chicken leg quarters

Herb Salt

   1 tablespoon sea salt

   1 teaspoon dried rosemary

   1/2 teaspoon dried thyme

   1/2 teaspoon cracked pepper

1 pound asparagus

1/2 yellow onion, thinly sliced

1. Preheat the oven to 375° F.

2. Melt the butter in a heavy cast iron skillet over medium-high heat until it starts to bubble.

3. Place the chicken leg quarters in the hot skillet, skin side down, and sear for 4 minutes per side. If you have a grill press or another heavy skillet, you can press the chicken legs down for a more effective sear.

4. Season the chicken leg quarters with the Herb Salt.

5. Chop the asparagus into 2-inch pieces, and place it in the skillet.

6. Add the onion to the skillet.

7. Lightly toss the vegetables with the juices in the pan, and cook for 15 minutes.

8. Lightly toss the vegetables with the juices again, and cook for another 20 minutes.

avocado and olive salad

[Serves 6]

Prep Time: 15 minutes } Total Time: 15 minutes : Difficulty: ⬤ ⬤ ⬤ ○ ○ : [1] [2] [3] [4]

5 cups spring mix salad greens

3/4 cup Kalamata olives

1 avocado, chopped

1/2 cup fresh cilantro, torn

Juice of 1/2 lemon

1/2 tablespoon olive oil

1 teaspoon dried rosemary

1 teaspoon dried sage

1/2 teaspoon salt

1. Place the mixed greens in a large salad bowl. Top the greens with the olives, avocado, and cilantro.

2. Drizzle the greens with lemon juice and olive oil.

3. Sprinkle with rosemary, sage, and salt.

4. Toss to combine all ingredients, and serve.

bacon, lettuce, and tomato salad

[Serves 4]

Prep Time: 5 minutes
Cook Time: 8 minutes } Total Time: 13 minutes

Difficulty: ● ● ○ ○ ○

1 **2** 3 **4**

3 strips bacon, cooked and crumbled

2 cups spring mix salad greens

1 Kumato tomato, thinly sliced

1/4 cup Kalamata olives

1 tablespoon fresh cilantro, torn

1. Cook the bacon in a cast iron skillet over medium-heat until crispy.

2. Remove the bacon from the skillet, and allow it to cool.

3. Add the mixed greens and sliced tomato to a large bowl.

4. Crumble the bacon over the salad, and top with Kalamata olives and torn cilantro leaves.

cobb salad

[Serves 2]

Prep Time: 15 minutes
Cook Time: 20 minutes } Total Time: 35 minutes

Difficulty: ● ○ ○ ○ ○

| 1 | 2 | 3 | 4 |

3 eggs

2 tablespoons coconut oil

1/2 pound chicken tenders

1 cup ham, cubed

1 Roma tomato, diced

1/2 cup cucumber, diced

1 avocado, diced

1 head green leaf lettuce, chopped

Dressing

   1/4 cup olive oil

   Juice of 1/2 lemon

   1/2 teaspoon salt

   1/2 teaspoon black pepper

1. Place the eggs in a saucepan with cool water. Bring the water to a boil, and cook the eggs for 10 minutes at a soft boil.

2. Remove the saucepan from the heat, pour off the boiling water, and replace with cool water and ice. Allow the eggs to cool.

3. Meanwhile, in a heavy skillet, heat the coconut oil over medium-high heat.

4. Add the chicken tenders to the skillet, and cook for 8-10 minutes, flipping occasionally to cook evenly.

5. Allow the chicken to rest for 5 minutes. Then, dice it, and set it aside.

6. Cube the ham, and dice the tomato, cucumber, and avocado. Set aside.

7. Chop the green leaf lettuce, and divide it equally between two large bowls.

8. Peel the eggs, and set them aside.

9. Top the lettuce with the chicken, ham, tomato, cucumber, avocado, and hard boiled egg.

10. In a small mixing bowl, make the dressing by whisking the olive oil, lemon juice, salt, and pepper. Pour the dressing over the individual salads.

cucumber noodle salad with tomato

[Serves 4]

Prep Time: 10 minutes } Total Time: 10 minutes   Difficulty: ● ○ ○ ○ ○   1 2 3 4

2 cups cucumber, julienned

2 cups grape tomatoes

1 clove garlic, minced

1 cup Kalamata olives

1 tablespoon basil, thinly sliced

1 tablespoon fresh oregano, chopped

2 tablespoons olive oil

2 tablespoons balsamic vinegar

1 teaspoon black pepper

1. Rinse and peel the cucumber. Use a julienne peeler to make noodles from the flesh of the cucumber, and stop when you get down to the seeds.

2. Rinse the grape tomatoes, and slice them in half.

3. In a medium-sized mixing bowl, toss the cucumber noodles, tomatoes, garlic, olives, basil, and oregano.

4. Drizzle the olive oil and balsamic vinegar over the salad, and sprinkle with black pepper.

grilled ahi tuna nicoise

[Serves 4]

Prep Time: 10 minutes
Cook Time: 25 minutes } Total Time: 35 minutes

Difficulty: ○ ○ ○ ○ ○

| 1 | 2 | 3 | 4 |

1 cup green beans, French-style, steamed

2 eggs

1 Ahi tuna steak (8 ounces)

1/4 teaspoon salt

1 teaspoon black pepper

2 tomatoes, quartered

1/2 cup Kalamata olives

2 teaspoons capers

4 cups spring mix salad greens

Dressing

   1/4 cup olive oil

   1/4 cup white balsamic vinegar

   1 tablespoon spicy brown mustard

   1/4 teaspoon salt

1. Steam the green beans until fork tender.

2. Meanwhile, place two eggs in a small saucepan, and cover them with water. Bring the water to a boil, and boil the eggs for 10 minutes.

3. When the eggs are cooked, immediately immerse them in an ice bath, peel, and allow them to cool completely.

4. While the eggs and green beans are cooling, preheat the grill to high-heat.

5. Sprinkle the tuna steak with salt and pepper on both sides.

6. Grill the tuna steak for 2 to 2 1/2 minutes per side. Remove the tuna from the grill, and slice.

7. Place the salad greens in a large bowl, and set aside.

8. Cut the eggs into quarters, and add the eggs, tomatoes, and green beans to the salad greens.

9. Top the salad with the olives and capers.

10. Carefully place the sliced tuna on top of the salad.

11. In a separate, small mixing bowl, whisk together the olive oil, vinegar, mustard, and salt, drizzle the dressing over the salad, and serve.

kale salad with bacon and fig vinaigrette

[Serves 2]

Prep Time: 5 minutes
Cook Time: 10 minutes } Total Time: 15 minutes

Difficulty: ● ● ○ ○ ○

1 2 3 4

2 large kale leaves

4 strips bacon

1 large red beet

2 radishes

1/2 teaspoon dried rosemary

3 cups spring mix salad greens

Dressing

  3 tablespoons olive oil

  1 1/2 tablespoons fig-infused balsamic vinegar (or any balsamic vinegar)

  1/2 teaspoon dried rosemary

1. Rinse the kale, and chop it into bite-sized pieces, removing the major veins. Set aside.

2. Heat a cast iron skillet on medium-heat.

3. Place the bacon in the skillet, and cook it until crisp. Remove the bacon and set aside.

4. Thinly slice the red beet and radishes using a vegetable peeler or mandoline slicer.

5. Sauté the beet ribbons in the bacon fat, with 1/2 teaspoon of dried rosemary, until soft. Set aside.

6. Toss the kale with the spring greens and radishes.

7. Top with the crumbled bacon and sautéed beets.

8. To make the dressing, whisk together the olive oil and fig-infused balsamic vinegar with 1/2 teaspoon of dried rosemary.

9. Drizzle the fig vinaigrette over the salad, and serve.

sesame-ginger flank steak salad

[Serves 4]

Prep Time: 15 minutes
Cook Time: 10 minutes } Total Time: 25 minutes

Difficulty: ● ● ● ○ ○

| 1 | 2 | 3 | 4 |

1 1/2 pounds flank steak

Salt and pepper to taste

1/2 pound asparagus

1/2 head green leaf lettuce

1 medium carrot, sliced

1 red bell pepper, sliced

1/2 cup Kalamata olives

Sesame-Ginger Dressing

  1/2 cup coconut aminos

  3 tablespoons toasted sesame

  oil

  1/2 teaspoon ground ginger

  1/4 teaspoon red pepper

  flakes

1. Preheat the grill to high-heat.

2. Season the steak liberally on both sides with salt and pepper.

3. Season the asparagus with salt.

4. When the grill has reached 500° F, place the steak and asparagus on it. Roll the asparagus occasionally to ensure even cooking.

5. Cook the steak for 3 minutes per side for medium-rare.

6. Allow the steak to rest for 5 minutes before slicing.

7. Assemble the salad with the green leaf lettuce, carrot, red bell pepper, and Kalamata olives.

8. Place the asparagus over the salad, and top with the steak.

9. To make the dressing, whisk together the coconut aminos, sesame oil, ground ginger, and red pepper flakes. Drizzle the dressing over the salad, and serve.

warm shrimp salad with bok choy

[Serves 4]

Prep Time: 5 minutes
Cook Time: 10 minutes } Total Time: 15 minutes   Difficulty: ⦿ ⦿ ⦿ ○ ○ | 1 | 2 | 3 | 4 |

1 large head bok choy

1/3 pound wild-caught shrimp,
   raw, peeled and deveined

1/4 teaspoon fish sauce

3 tablespoons coconut aminos

2 cloves garlic, minced

1/4 cup watercress

1. Heat a large skillet over medium-high heat.

2. Rinse the bok choy, and remove the large white veins near the bottom of each leaf. Chop the leaves lengthwise, and set aside.

3. Place the shrimp in the skillet, and stir in the fish sauce and coconut aminos. Sauté for 4-5 minutes.

4. Add the minced garlic and watercress, and continue to sauté until the shrimp is completely opaque.

5. Add the bok choy, and sauté 1-2 minutes, until it begins to soften slightly.

6. Remove the skillet from the heat, and serve immediately.

asparagus with gremolata

[Serves 4]

Prep Time: 5 minutes
Cook Time: 30 minutes } Total Time: 35 minutes

Difficulty: ● ○ ○ ○ ○

1 **2** 3 4

2 pounds asparagus, rinsed and
ends removed

Salt and pepper to taste

1 tablespoon duck fat

Gremolata

1 bunch flat leaf parsley, finely
chopped

Juice and zest of 1/2 lemon

1 clove garlic, minced

Salt and pepper to taste

1. Preheat the oven to 400° F.

2. Place the asparagus in a baking dish, season with salt and pepper, and top with the duck fat.

3. Place the asparagus in the hot oven for 5 minutes. Then, remove, stir, and place it back in the oven to cook for another 25-30 minutes.

4. Meanwhile, to begin the Gremolata, rinse the parsley under cool water, and pat dry thoroughly.

5. Finely chop the parsley, and place it in a medium-sized mixing bowl.

6. Add the juice and zest of half a lemon, the minced garlic, salt, and pepper to the bowl, and stir to combine all ingredients.

7. Remove the asparagus from the oven, top it with the Gremolata, and serve.

bacon-y sweet potato hash

[Serves 4]

Prep Time: 10 minutes
Cook Time: 25 minutes } Total Time: 35 minutes

Difficulty: ● ● ○ ○ ○

1 2 3 4

3 large sweet potatoes

5 strips bacon

4 tablespoons lard or bacon fat

1 tablespoon salt

1 teaspoon pepper

Salt and pepper to taste

1. Peel the sweet potatoes, and grate them on a coarse setting using a food processor or box grater. Set aside.

2. Chop the bacon into 1-inch pieces.

3. Heat a large Dutch oven or soup pot over medium-heat, and fry the bacon. Then, remove it from the pot, leaving the bacon fat.

4. Add an additional 4 tablespoons of lard to the pot, and allow it to melt.

5. Add the shredded sweet potatoes to the pot, and stir to evenly disperse the fat.

6. Cook the sweet potatoes over medium-heat, tossing occasionally to cook evenly.

7. Add the salt to season and help draw out the moisture from the sweet potatoes. Cook for approximately 15 minutes.

8. Near the end of cooking, stir in the cooked bacon.

9. Season with a bit of salt and pepper, and serve.

brussels sprouts with bacon and dates

[Serves 2]

Prep Time: 5 minutes
Cook Time: 25 minutes } Total Time: 30 minutes : Difficulty: ● ○ ○ ○ ○ : 1 2 3 4

2 strips bacon, chopped

3 cups Brussels sprouts, sliced

1 cup Medjool dates

Salt and pepper to taste

1. Heat a heavy skillet over medium-heat. Place the strips of bacon in the skillet, and cook them until crispy.

2. Add the Brussels sprouts to the skillet, and sauté them until soft.

3. Add the dates, and sauté for 5 minutes.

4. Season with salt and pepper, and serve.

buttered squash ribbons

[Serves 2]

Prep Time: 10 minutes
Cook Time: 10 minutes } Total Time: 20 minutes ⋮ Difficulty: ◉ ○ ○ ○ ○ ⋮ 1 2 3 4

2 medium yellow squash

2 medium zucchini

1 tablespoon grass-fed butter

Salt and pepper to taste

2 tablespoons fresh oregano,

chopped

2 tablespoons fresh basil,

chopped

1. Using a vegetable peeler, slice the squash and zucchini into ribbons. Stop when you reach the seeds, and discard the core.

2. Heat the butter in a skillet over medium-high heat.

3. Add the squash ribbons and sauté, tossing to evenly coat with butter.

4. Sprinkle the squash with the salt, pepper, oregano, and basil. Continue to sauté until the squash is tender.

cabbage with onions and apples

[Serves 4]

Prep Time: 10 minutes
Cook Time: 45-60 minutes } Total Time: 1 hour

Difficulty: ◉ ○ ○ ○ ○

1 **2** 3 4

1 head green cabbage, shredded

2 green apples, cored and thinly sliced

1 small yellow onion, thinly sliced

2 tablespoons duck fat

Salt and pepper to taste

1. Preheat the oven to 400° F.

2. Place the shredded cabbage in a large baking dish.

3. Top the cabbage with the onion and apples.

4. Season with salt and pepper, and stir to combine all ingredients.

5. Top with duck fat, and place the dish in the oven for 5 minutes. Remove from the oven, and stir to combine the veggies with the melted fat.

6. Place the veggies back in the oven, and bake for an additional 45-60 minutes, stirring every 20 minutes to prevent burning on the surface.

homemade mayonnaise

[Makes 1.5 cups]

Prep Time: 10 minutes } Total Time: 10 minutes ⋮ Difficulty: ● ● ○ ○ ○ ⋮ 1 2 3 4

1 egg

1 tablespoon lemon juice

1/4 teaspoon ground yellow
   mustard seed

1/3 cup coconut oil, melted

1/3 cup olive oil

1/3 cup sesame oil

1/2 teaspoon black pepper

1/2 teaspoon salt

1. In a blender or food processor, blend the egg, lemon juice, and ground mustard seed.

2. Melt the coconut oil gently, so that it is cool but still liquid. Coconut oil melts at 75° F.

3. In a small separate bowl, stir together the coconut oil, olive oil, and sesame oil until they are evenly combined.

4. Add the oil mixture to the food processor 1 tablespoon at a time—the slower, the better. Typically, the full amount of oil takes 3-4 minutes to add.

5. When the oil has all emulsified and you have a creamy mayonnaise, add the salt and pepper, and continue to blend.

roasted cauliflower with caper relish

[Serves 4]

Prep Time: 10 minutes
Cook Time: 40 minutes } Total Time: 50 minutes   Difficulty: ● ● ● ○ ○   1 2 3 4

1 head cauliflower

1 tablespoon duck fat, melted

Salt and pepper to taste

Caper Relish

   2 tablespoons grass-fed butter, unsalted

   1 clove garlic, smashed and chopped

   1/4 cup capers

   Juice of 1 lemon

   Crushed black pepper to taste

1. Preheat the oven to 425° F.

2. Chop the cauliflower into florets, and place it in a rimmed baking dish with the melted duck fat. Toss to coat, and season with salt and pepper.

3. Roast for 35-40 minutes.

4. With 10 minutes of cooking left to go, start the Caper Relish by melting the butter over medium-heat in a small saucepan or skillet.

5. Add the garlic, and sauté for about 1 minute.

6. Add the capers, lemon juice, and crushed black pepper.

7. When the mixture starts to bubble, cook for 1 final minute, and remove from the heat.

8. Serve the cauliflower topped with the Caper Relish.

roasted delicata squash

[Serves 4]

Prep Time: 5 minutes
Cook Time: 45-60 minutes } Total Time: 50-65 minutes

Difficulty: ◉ ○ ○ ○ ○   1 2 3 4

1 delicata squash

1 tablespoon grass-fed butter,

  unsalted

1/2 teaspoon salt

1/2 teaspoon pepper

1/2 teaspoon cinnamon

1. Preheat the oven to 400° F.

2. Cut the delicata squash in half, lengthwise and scoop out seeds.

3. Place 1/2 tablespoon of butter on each half of the squash.

4. Sprinkle it with salt, pepper, and cinnamon, and place the squash in a baking dish. Cook for 45-60 minutes, until fork tender.

roasted rosemary carrots with onion

[Serves 8]

Prep Time: 20 minutes
Cook Time: 60 minutes } Total Time: 80 minutes   Difficulty: ⬤ ⬤ ⬤ ○ ○   1 2 3 4

10 large carrots, peeled and

chopped

1 large yellow onion, chopped

1 tablespoon dried rosemary

Salt and pepper to taste

1 tablespoon grass-fed butter,

unsalted

1. Preheat the oven to 400° F.

2. Combine the carrots and onion in a large baking dish.

3. Season them with rosemary, salt, and pepper. Top with grass-fed butter.

4. Place the vegetables in the oven for 5 minutes.

5. Remove, and stir to combine the veggies with the melted butter.

6. Return the carrots to the oven, and roast for 45-60 minutes, stirring every 20 minutes until the carrots are tender.

smoky roasted turnips with bacon

[Serves 4]

Prep Time: 20 minutes
Cook Time: 60 minutes } Total Time: 80 minutes

Difficulty: ● ● ○ ○ ○

1 2 3 4

4 turnips, ends removed and chopped into bite-sized pieces

2 tablespoons bacon grease, melted

1 teaspoon smoked paprika

1 teaspoon garlic powder

1 teaspoon salt

1 teaspoon black pepper

1 strip bacon, cooked and chopped to garnish

1. Preheat the oven to 425° F.

2. Place the turnips in an oven-safe baking dish, and toss with the melted bacon grease.

3. Sprinkle with smoked paprika, garlic powder, salt, and pepper. Toss to evenly coat.

4. Bake uncovered for 30 minutes, stirring every so often to ensure even cooking.

5. After 30 minutes, turn the heat down to 350° F, move the turnips to a lower rack, and place the bacon in the oven to bake on a wire rack over a cookie sheet.

6. Remove the turnips after the bacon has baked for 10-15 minutes, but check periodically to ensure that the turnips are not burning.

7. Once the bacon is crisp (about 25-30 minutes), remove it from the oven, chop it, and place it on the turnips before serving.

spicy garden salsa

[Serves 4]

Prep Time: 15 minutes } Total Time: 15 minutes   Difficulty: ● ○ ○ ○ ○   1 2 3 4

1/3 cup green bell pepper, finely

  diced

1/3 cup diced Roma tomatoes

1/3 cup diced yellow tomatoes

Juice of 1/2 lime

2 tablespoons olive oil

1/2 teaspoon salt

1/4 teaspoon black pepper

1/8 teaspoon chipotle powder, or

  to taste

1 cucumber, sliced into chips, or

  Belgian endive or celery sticks

1. Place the diced pepper and tomatoes in a large bowl.

2. Drizzle with the juice of 1/2 lime and the olive oil.

3. Add the salt, pepper, and chipotle powder.

4. Serve with thin slices of cucumber, Belgian endive, or celery sticks.

tomato bacon casserole

[Serves 4]

Prep Time: 10 minutes
Cook Time: 45 minutes } Total Time: 55 minutes : Difficulty: ⬤ ⬤ ⬤ ◯ ◯ : 1 2 3 4

3 tablespoons grass-fed butter, unsalted

3 strips bacon, chopped

1 small yellow onion

2 medium vine-ripe tomatoes

2 medium yellow tomatoes

1 teaspoon dried rosemary

1 teaspoon dried oregano

1/2 teaspoon salt

1. Preheat the oven to 350° F.

2. Place 2 tablespoons of the butter in a skillet over medium-high heat.

3. Once the butter is hot and starts to bubble, add the chopped bacon to the skillet.

4. Slice the onion, and add it to the bacon when the bacon is crispy. Sauté the onion until soft.

5. Thinly slice the tomatoes.

6. Lightly grease a 4-cup casserole dish, and line the bottom with a layer of the tomato slices.

7. Spoon some of the bacon and onion mixture over the tomatoes. Repeat layering, ending with the tomatoes on top.

8. Sprinkle the dish with the rosemary, oregano, and salt.

9. Chop the remaining 1 tablespoon of butter, and place it on top of the tomatoes.

10. Bake for 40 minutes until the butter bubbles and the tomatoes are golden on top.

beef brisket

[Serves 4]

Prep Time: 20 minutes
Cook Time: 5 hours } Total Time: 5.5 hours

Difficulty: ● ● ○ ○ ○

| 1 | 2 | **3** | 4 |

1 yellow onion, chopped

2 pounds beef brisket

1/2 teaspoon salt

1/2 pepper

2 teaspoons dried basil

2 teaspoons dried oregano

1 can tomato sauce, no salt added
  (15 ounces)

1. Preheat oven to 350° F.

2. Cover the bottom of a braising pan with the chopped onion.

3. Place the brisket over the chopped onion.

4. Sprinkle the brisket on all sides with salt, pepper, basil and oregano.

5. Place the brisket in the oven and cook uncovered for 1 hour.

6. Reduce the oven temperature to 325° F.

7. Pour the tomato sauce over the brisket, sprinkle again with additional salt, pepper, basil and oregano.

8. Cover the braising pan with a lid, and cook for a remaining 4 hours at 325° F.

braised beef shanks

[Serves 2]

Prep Time: 20 minutes
Cook Time: 2 hours } Total Time: 2.5 hours

Difficulty: ⬤ ⬤ ◯ ◯ ◯

| 1 | 2 | 3 | 4 |

4 beef shanks

1 1/2 tablespoons coconut oil, divided

1 head garlic, half the cloves smashed and chopped, the other half sliced in half to stud, divided

1 handful fresh thyme sprigs

1 cup Beef Bone Broth (page 196)

1/2 cup water

1/2 teaspoon salt or to taste

1/2 teaspoon pepper or to taste

1. Preheat the oven to 350° F.

2. Rinse the beef shanks under cold water, and pat them dry.

3. Sprinkle the beef shanks with salt and pepper on both sides.

4. Heat 1/2 tablespoon of the coconut oil in a cast iron skillet on medium-high heat. Sear the beef shanks in the coconut oil for 2-3 minutes per side, adding a bit more coconut oil to the skillet as needed for each additional shank.

5. Place the seared shanks in a glass baking dish, and set aside.

6. Sauté the smashed/chopped garlic and thyme leaves in the skillet for about 1 minute.

7. Add the broth and 1/2 cup of water to the skillet, and stir, making sure to scrape any of the brown bits from the shanks on the bottom.

8. Bring the liquid to a boil until it starts to reduce slightly.

9. Place the remaining garlic cloves and additional thyme springs in the pan with the beef shanks.

10. Pour the broth over the beef shanks.

11. Cover the meat with parchment paper and then aluminum foil.

12. Bake for 2 hours.

beef tagine

[Serves 4-6]

Prep Time: 20 minutes
Cook Time: 3-4 hours } Total Time: 3-4 hours

Difficulty: ● ● ● ○ ○

| 1 | 2 | 3 | 4 |

1 tablespoon coconut oil

5 medium carrots, chopped

5 stalks of celery, chopped

1 vidalia onion, chopped

1 cup white mushrooms

2 lbs beef stew meat

1 cup strained tomatoes

Salt and pepper to taste

1 bay leaf

1 teaspoon cinnamon

1 teaspoon cumin

1 teaspoon garlic powder

1 teaspoon paprika

1. Warm the coconut oil over medium-heat in a tagine or medium soup pot.

2. Sauté the carrots, celery, onion, and white mushrooms over medium-heat for 2 minutes.

3. Add the beef stew meat to the tagine.

4. Pour the strained tomatoes over everything. Season with salt and pepper, and add the bay leaf.

5. Turn the heat down to low, cover, and simmer for 1 hour.

6. Add the spices to the dish, stir to mix, and continue to cook covered for an additional 2-3 hours.

pressure cooker pork roast

[Serves 6]

Prep Time: 10 minutes
Cook Time: 45 minutes } Total Time: 55 minutes

Difficulty: ● ○ ○ ○ ○

| 1 | 2 | 3 | 4 |

6 carrots, chopped

1 whole yellow onion, chopped

6 celery stalks, chopped

3-4 pounds pork roast

1 teaspoon onion powder

1 teaspoon garlic powder

1 teaspoon cinnamon

1 teaspoon dried marjoram

1 teaspoon salt

1 teaspoon pepper

1/2 teaspoon nutmeg

1. Place the carrots, onion, and celery in the bottom of a pressure cooker, and add 1 cup of water.

2. Rinse the pork roast, and pat dry.

3. Rub the pork roast with the onion powder, garlic powder, cinnamon, dried marjoram, salt, pepper, and nutmeg, and place the meat in the pressure cooker.

4. Cook the pork roast on high pressure for 45 minutes. Carefully release the pressure, allowing all steam to escape before unlocking the pot lid.

5. Alternately, you can slow cook this dish in a crock pot on low for 8-10 hours.

rump roast under pressure

[Serves 4]

Prep Time: 15 minutes
Cook Time: 60 minutes } Total Time: 75 minutes

Difficulty: ● ○ ○ ○ ○

1 2 3 **4**

3 1/2 pounds beef rump roast

2 tablespoons duck fat or lard

15 cloves garlic, peeled

2 tablespoons Adobo Seasoning
(page 212)

2 cups Beef Bone Broth (page 196)

1. Rinse the rump roast, and pat it dry.

2. Heat the duck fat or lard in a pressure cooker* over medium-high heat.

3. In a skillet, sear the rump roast on all sides.

4. Using a short, sharp knife, make 1-inch incisions into the beef, and "stud" it with the garlic cloves.

5. Season the beef liberally with the Adobo Seasoning.

6. Pour the beef broth into the pressure cooker, and place the rump roast into the pressure cooker.

7. Cook on high pressure for 1 hour. Carefully release the pressure, allowing all steam to escape before unlocking the pot lid.

8. Remove, allow to rest for 5 minutes, slice, and serve.

* If you don't have a pressure cooker, you can make this recipe in the oven by studding and seasoning the rump roast, and placing it in a roasting pan. Sear the rump roast at 500° F for 20 minutes. Then, finish cooking it at 325° F, allotting 30 minutes per pound or until the internal temperature reads 120-125° F for rare, 130-140° F for medium-rare.

tomato braised short ribs

[Serves 6]

Prep Time: 15 minutes
Cook Time: 8 hours } Total Time: 8 hours

Difficulty: ⬤ ⬤ ⬤ ◯ ◯   1 2 **3** 4

1 tablespoon bacon grease

5 pounds beef short ribs

1 teaspoon salt or to taste

1 teaspoon pepper or to taste

1 tablespoon dried basil

10 cloves garlic, smashed

2 15 ounce cans tomato sauce, no

salt added

1. Heat the bacon grease in a cast iron skillet over high-heat.

2. Sear the short ribs about 1 minute per side or just until they are browned well. Then, place them in a large crock pot.

3. Sprinkle the ribs generously with salt and pepper, and top with dried basil.

4. Place the smashed garlic over the ribs.

5. Pour two cans of tomato sauce over the ribs, cover the crock pot, and cook on low for 7 hours.

6. Remove the lid and, if the sauce seems soupy, turn the crock pot to high for 1 additional hour of cooking before serving.

bison stew

[Serves 8]

Prep Time: 20 minutes
Cook Time: 6-8 hours } Total Time: 6-8 hours

Difficulty: ● ● ● ○ ○

| 1 | 2 | **3** | 4 |

2 pounds bison steak medallions

1 tablespoon coconut oil

1 yellow onion, chopped

2 cups celery, chopped, reserving the greens

6 cups Beef Bone Broth (page 196)

1/2 teaspoon salt or to taste

1/2 teaspoon pepper or to taste

3 sprigs thyme

3 sprigs fresh rosemary

1 head cauliflower, chopped

1. In a cast iron skillet, brown the bison stew meat on all sides in the coconut oil.

2. Transfer the seared bison meat into a large soup pot.

3. Place the chopped onion and celery into the pot with the bison, and pour the beef broth over the meat.

4. Season the meat liberally with salt and pepper.

5. Add the thyme, rosemary, and celery greens to the pot, and turn the burner to medium-heat.

6. Bring the stew to a boil, stirring often.

7. Once the stew comes to a boil, reduce the heat to low, and cover.

8. Simmer the stew for 6-8 hours, adding the chopped cauliflower for the last hour of cooking.

bone broth (beef or chicken)

[Yields 6-8 cups]

Prep Time: 5 minutes
Cook Time: 1 hour } Total Time: 1 hour

Difficulty: ● ○ ○ ○ ○ | 1 | 2 | 3 | 4 |

4 pounds grass-fed beef bones or

chicken backs and feet

Filtered water

1 tablespoon Himalayan sea salt

1 tablespoon apple cider vinegar

1. Place the beef bones or chicken backs in a pressure cooker*.

2. Cover the bones with filtered water, and add the Himalayan sea salt and apple cider vinegar.

3. Lock the lid in place, heat to high pressure, and cook for 1 hour.

4. Strain out the bones and any particles before using as soup stock.

* If you do not have a pressure cooker, you can cook the bone broth on low for 16-24 hours in a slow cooker (crock pot).

broccoli and leek soup

[Serves 6]

Prep Time: 20 minutes
Cook Time: 15 minutes } Total Time: 35 minutes | Difficulty: ⬤ ⬤ ◯ ◯ ◯ | 1 2 **3** 4

1 tablespoon duck fat

1 cup leek, sliced

2 cloves garlic, minced

Salt and pepper to taste

1 head broccoli

5 cups Chicken Bone Broth (page 196)

Green onion slices for garnish

1. Heat the duck fat in a heavy skillet over medium-heat.

2. Place the leek in the skillet, and sauté it until soft.

3. Add the minced garlic to the skillet, and continue to sauté lightly, adding salt and pepper to taste.

4. In a saucepan, boil the head of broccoli in water until fork tender.

5. In a food processor, purée the chicken broth with the broccoli and leek until evenly combined.

6. Add all ingredients to a stock pot, and heat over medium-heat until hot.

7. Season with salt and pepper, and garnish with sliced green onion.

chicken soup with bone broth

[Yeild 3 quarts]

Prep Time: 15 minutes
Cook Time: 30 hours } Total Time: 30 hours*

Difficulty: ● ● ○ ○ ○   1 2 3 **4**

*Bone broth takes 24 hours in a crock pot or 1 hour in a pressure cooker.
*Soup takes an additional 4-6 hours once the broth is made.

3 quarts Chicken Bone Broth

1 chicken carcass (with neck)

2 quarts purified water

1 tablespoon Himalayan sea salt

2 tablespoons apple cider vinegar

16 boneless skinless chicken thighs

1 yellow onion, chopped

4 large carrots, chopped

1 celery heart, chopped

1/2 tablespoon sea salt

1 teaspoon black pepper

1 tablespoon dill weed

1. Place the chicken carcass, Himalayan sea salt, and apple cider vinegar in a crock pot. Fill it with purified water.

2. Cook on low for 24 hours to make the bone broth. In lieu of slow cooking, this can also be made using a pressure cooker. Cook on high pressure for 1 hour.

3. Remove the bones, and strain the broth with a fine mesh sieve to remove any remaining bones or meat. Store any extra broth frozen for up to 3 months or refrigerated for 1 week.

4. To make the soup, place the chicken thighs in a crock pot.

5. Chop the onion, carrots, and celery into bite-sized pieces, and place them into a crock pot.

6. Add the bone broth, salt, pepper, and dill to the crock pot.

7. Cook the soup on low for 4-6 hours.

cream of mushroom soup

[Serves 4]

Prep Time: 20 minutes
Cook Time: 60 minutes } Total Time: 80 minutes ⁞ Difficulty: ● ● ○ ○ ○ ⁞ 1 2 3 4

2 tablespoons grass-fed butter, coconut oil, or duck fat

1 small yellow onion, diced

16 ounces sliced white mushrooms, chopped

2 cloves garlic, minced

Salt and pepper to taste

1 teaspoon dried thyme leaves

1 cup full-fat coconut milk

3 cups Chicken Bone Broth (page 196)

1. In a large soup pot, melt the butter over medium-heat. Add the onion to the pot, and sauté for 1 minute.

2. Add the chopped mushrooms and the garlic to the pot, and continue to sauté until the mushrooms start to soften.

3. Season with salt, pepper, and dried thyme leaves.

4. Sauté the onion and mushrooms for 10 more minutes, and add the coconut milk.

5. Bring the coconut milk to a bubbling boil, and add the Chicken Bone Broth.

6. Stir the soup well, bringing it to a boil.

7. Reduce the soup to a simmer, cover, and simmer for 1 hour.

italian wedding soup

[Serves 8]

Prep Time: 30 minutes
Cook Time: 75 minutes } Total Time: 1 1/2 hours   Difficulty: ◉ ◯ ◯ ◯ ◯ | 1 | 2 | 3 | 4 |

2 pounds ground pork

2 teaspoons salt

2 teaspoons pepper

1 tablespoon garlic powder

1 tablespoon onion powder

2 teaspoons dried oregano

8 cups Chicken Bone Broth (page 196)

2 medium carrots, chopped

3 celery stalks, chopped

1 head escarole

1. Place the ground pork in a large mixing bowl, and season with the salt, pepper, garlic powder, onion powder, and oregano. Mix thoroughly to evenly combine.

2. Roll the ground pork into 1/2-inch meatballs. Set them aside to add to the soup later.

3. In a large soup pot, bring the Chicken Bone Broth to a boil.

4. Add the chopped carrots and celery.

5. Once the broth has reached a rolling boil, add the meatballs slowly and carefully. Adding too many cold meatballs at once will cool the soup.

6. Allow the meatballs to boil for 10 minutes.

7. Lightly chop the escarole, and add to the soup.

8. Reduce the heat to low, cover, and simmer for 1 hour.

pressure cooker beef stew

[Serves 12]

Prep Time: 15 minutes
Cook Time: 1 hour } Total Time: 75 minutes

Difficulty: ● ● ○ ○ ○

| 1 | 2 | 3 | 4 |

6 cups Beef Bone Broth (page 196)

6 large carrots, chopped

1/2 celery heart, chopped

1 small yellow onion, chopped

3 cloves garlic, smashed

3 pounds grass-fed beef stew meat

1 can diced tomatoes (15 ounces)

Salt and pepper to taste

1. Make the Beef Bone Broth on page 196. With the beef stock in a large pressure cooker, add the carrots, celery, onion, garlic, stew meat, and diced tomatoes.

2. Season with salt and pepper, lock the lid in place, and cook on high pressure for 1 hour.

*If you do not own a pressure cooker, you can cook this stew in a soup pot by bringing the stew to a boil, then reducing heat, covering, and simmering for 2-4 hours.

express eats: protein

SAUSAGE PATTIES

Sausage patties are a great way to enjoy a flavorful breakfast food with very little effort. All you need is a pound of pastured ground meat (your choice) and a few tablespoons of your favorite sausage spice blend. Typically, sausage is made with pork, but you can use ground beef, chicken, or lamb and still enjoy a flavorful sausage! Mix the spices with the ground meat, form into 2-ounce patties, and bake in the oven for 25-30 minutes at 350° F.

SAUTÉED SHRIMP

Here's one of our favorite quick and easy seafood meals: A pound or two of wild-caught shrimp fried in a skillet with vegetables and coconut aminos. Shrimp cooks really fast, so add the shrimp last. Throw your cooking oil and colorful veggies into a skillet, and once the veggies are just about finished cooking, add the shrimp. Season with black pepper, a pinch of salt, and coconut aminos, and, presto—a fantastic meal in no time at all!

BROWNED BEEF WITH VEGETABLES

This is an easy, affordable meal that is also extremely flavorful. All you need are your favorite veggies and your choices of cooking fat and grass-fed ground meat. Melt your cooking fat in a large skillet, and add vegetables. Once your vegetables are soft, add your meat. Sauté until the meat is brown, and season as desired. Breakfast, lunch, or dinner will be finished before you know it!

BAKED CHICKEN THIGHS

Another mouth-watering favorite. Grab a pack of air-chilled organic chicken thighs (bone in, skin on), season with salt and pepper, and bake for 45 minutes at 425° F. The skin on the chicken gets super crispy, and the meat is extremely juicy. We pair chicken thighs with salad, roasted green vegetables, cauliflower purée, and roasted sweet potatoes. There are countless sides you can try with this versatile dish.

GRILLED MEAT

We love grilling and eating al fresco in the summer months. Our favorites are grass-fed rib eye steaks, baby back ribs, salmon filets, and a vegetable mix of broccoli, bell peppers, asparagus, mushrooms, and onions. For perfectly grilled meat, bring your meat out of the refrigerator 20 minutes prior to cooking and season with salt and pepper. Heat the grill to high-heat. When the grill has reached 500° F, sear the meat on each side. When the meat easily releases from the cooking surface, it has been seared. Reduce the heat, and cook until the desired internal temperature is reached.

MEATBALLS

Meatballs are as simple as sausage patties. Season your choice of ground meat as desired, form into 1-2-ounce meatballs, and bake for 25-30 minutes at 350° F. We toss meatballs into a salad or throw them over roasted spaghetti squash and pureed vegetables. They also make for delicious finger food when you're on the go!

1

2

3

4

5

6

Hayley Mason and Bill Staley

express eats: vegetables

SAUTÉED MUSHROOMS

We love all vegetables sautéed. It's a fast way to get a ton of colorful veggies into your diet. We like to cook mushrooms on top of the stove. For a really flavorful dish, sauté in grass-fed butter or coconut oil, and throw in a sprig or two of rosemary along with some chopped onion—a perfect topping for steaks, burgers, or roast chicken.

ROASTED BROCCOLI

Roasted broccoli is the simplest side dish for any meal, and our favorite at home. Chop up organic broccoli florets, season with herb salt, top with a pat or two of grass-fed butter, duck fat, or coconut oil, and bake for 30 minutes at 400° F. After 5 minutes of cooking, we remove the broccoli from the oven to stir the melted fat.

GRILLED VEGETABLE MEDLEY

Nothing makes us happier than filling our grill basket with a colorful array of our homegrown vegetables: broccoli, asparagus, mushrooms, red and orange bell peppers, carrots, purple onions, and even eggplant. Toss the veggies with your choice of melted cooking fat in a mixing bowl, season with salt and pepper, and grill until they've caramelized in the smoky heat. For a truly epic meal, serve alongside your favorite grilled steak.

SALAD

We love salad, especially in the warmer months, and there are so many ways to spice them up. Our favorite salad is organic greens, avocado, olives, cucumber, and olive oil with lemon juice. We never get tired of that one. But you can add carrots and tomatoes, top with grilled or roasted meat, or add some egg and ham. Berries, apples, pears, and citrus are all fruits that work beautifully in green salads.

FRIED GREEN CABBAGE

This is one of our favorite breakfast sides, and it couldn't be simpler to make: Thinly slice a head of organic green cabbage, and stir-fry it in coconut oil, salt, and pepper. The cabbage will be finished cooking when it becomes soft and flexible. It's super flavorful and perfect with pastured eggs. Nothing sops up the runny yolk of a fried egg better than cabbage! Top with some sliced avocado, and you are set.

MASHED CAULIFLOWER

This is for when you're missing mashed potatoes. All you need is a head of cauliflower, a pot of water, a high-speed blender or food processor, and your favorite herb salt blend. Steam or boil the cauliflower florets until fork tender, drain, place in a high-speed blender or food processor, season with herbs and salt, and purée until smooth and fluffy. Top with a braised or roasted meat, and you have yourself some super simple comfort food. Who knows? You might even like it better than potatoes!

Hayley Mason and Bill Staley

express eats: spice mixes

1. ADOBO SEASONING

- 6 tablespoons salt
- 6 tablespoons granulated garlic
- 4 tablespoons oregano
- 2 tablespoons black pepper
- 2 tablespoons onion powder

2. SAUSAGE SEASONING

- 1 teaspoon garlic powder
- 1 teaspoon paprika
- 1/2 teaspoon rubbed sage
- 1 teaspoon fennel seeds
- 1/4 teaspoon cayenne pepper
- 1/4 teaspoon white pepper
- 1/2 teaspoon salt
- 1/2 teaspoon black pepper

3. COFFEE RUB

- 1 tablespoon ground coffee
- 1 tablespoon salt
- 1 tablespoon granulated garlic
- 2 teaspoons oregano
- 2 teaspoons black pepper
- 2 teaspoons onion powder

4. BBQ BLEND SPICE MIX

- 1 teaspoon smoked paprika
- 1 teaspoon onion powder
- 1 teaspoon garlic powder
- 1 teaspoon chipotle powder
- 1 teaspoon cinnamon
- 1 teaspoon coriander
- 1 teaspoon black pepper

5. TACO SEASONING

- 2 tablespoons chili powder
- 1 1/2 tablespoons cumin
- 1 1/2 tablespoons paprika
- 1 tablespoon onion powder
- 1 tablespoon garlic powder
- 2 teaspoons oregano
- 1/2 teaspoon red pepper flakes

6. CREOLE SEASONING

- 1 tablespoon paprika
- 1 tablespoon salt
- 2 teaspoons ground black pepper
- 1 teaspoon cayenne powder
- 2 teaspoons garlic powder
- 2 teaspoons onion powder
- 2 teaspoons dried thyme
- 1 teaspoon dried oregano

Hayley Mason and Bill Staley

express eats: sauces and marinades

HAYLEY'S MARINADE

- 1 teaspoon dried basil
- 1 teaspoon dried oregano
- 1/4 cup extra-virgin olive oil
- 2 cloves garlic, minced
- 1/2 lemon, juice only
- 1/2 teaspoon black pepper
- 1/2 teaspoon salt

FIG BALSAMIC DRESSING

- 1/2 cup extra-virgin olive oil
- 1/4 cup fig balsamic vinegar
- 2 teaspoons spicy brown mustard
- 1/2 teaspoon Himalayan salt
- 1/2 teaspoon dried marjoram
- 1/2 teaspoon ground black pepper

TANGY TERIYAKI

- 1/2 cup coconut aminos
- 1/4 cup spicy brown mustard
- 3 cloves garlic, pressed
- 1 teaspoon Himalayan salt
- 1 teaspoon paprika

CHIMICHURRI

- 1 cup flat leaf parsley
- 3 cloves garlic, chopped
- 2 lemons, juice only
- 1/2 cup extra-virgin olive oil
- 1 teaspoon salt
- 1 teaspoon black pepper
- 1/4 teaspoon red pepper flakes

CITRUS MARINADE

- 1 tablespoon spicy brown mustard
- 1 tablespoon white balsamic raspberry blush vinegar
- 4 cloves garlic, minced
- 1 orange, juice only
- 3 limes, juice only

SESAME-GINGER DRESSING

- 1/2 cup coconut aminos
- 3 tablespoons toasted sesame oil
- 1/2 teaspoon ground ginger
- 1/4 teaspoon red pepper flakes

Hayley Mason and Bill Staley

Table of Conversions

VOLUMES

US	Metric
1 tsp	5 ml
1 tbsp (1/2 fl oz)	15 ml
1/4 cup (2 fl oz)	60 ml
1/3 cup	80 ml
1/2 cup (4 fl oz)	120 ml
2/3 cup	160 ml
3/4 cup (6 fl oz)	180 ml
1 cup (8 fl oz)	240 ml
1 qt (32 fl oz)	950 ml
1 qt + 3 tbsps	1 L
1 gal (128 fl oz)	4 L

WEIGHTS

US	Metric
1/4 oz	7 g
1/2 oz	15 g
3/4 oz	20 g
1 oz	30 g
8 oz (1/2 lb)	225 g
12 oz (3/4 lb)	340 g
16 oz (1 lb)	455 g
35 oz (2.2 lbs)	1 kg

TEMPERATURES

Fahrenheit	Celsius
0°	-18°
32°	0°
180°	82°
212°	100°
250°	120°
350°	175°
425°	220°
500°	260

All temperatures in book are noted in Fahrenheit

Index [ingredients and recipes]

Index [general topics]

Week 1 Meal Plan

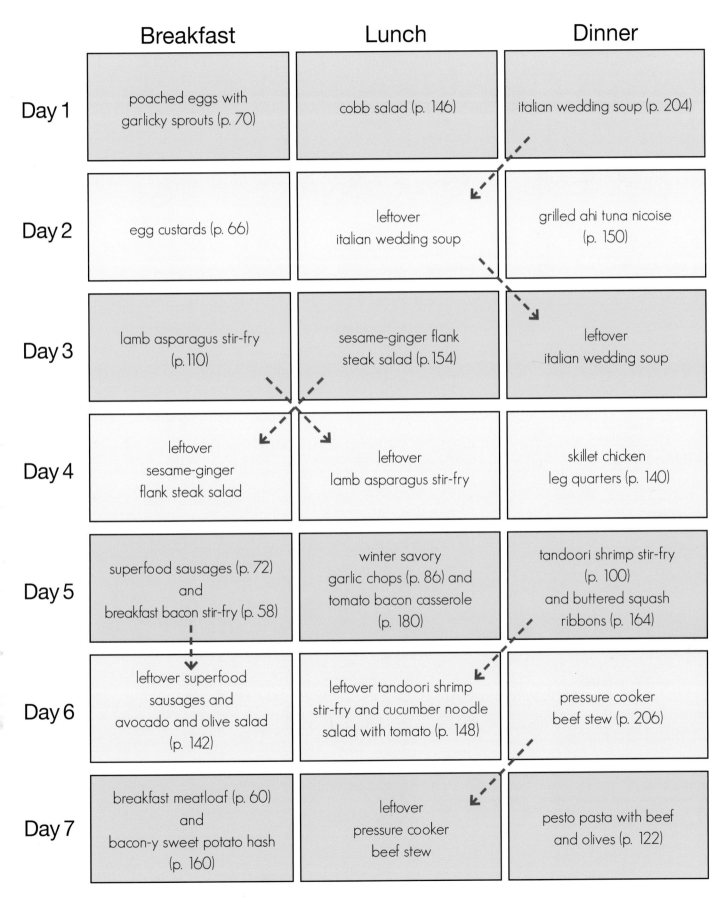

	Breakfast	Lunch	Dinner
Day 1	poached eggs with garlicky sprouts (p. 70)	cobb salad (p. 146)	italian wedding soup (p. 204)
Day 2	egg custards (p. 66)	leftover italian wedding soup	grilled ahi tuna nicoise (p. 150)
Day 3	lamb asparagus stir-fry (p. 110)	sesame-ginger flank steak salad (p. 154)	leftover italian wedding soup
Day 4	leftover sesame-ginger flank steak salad	leftover lamb asparagus stir-fry	skillet chicken leg quarters (p. 140)
Day 5	superfood sausages (p. 72) and breakfast bacon stir-fry (p. 58)	winter savory garlic chops (p. 86) and tomato bacon casserole (p. 180)	tandoori shrimp stir-fry (p. 100) and buttered squash ribbons (p. 164)
Day 6	leftover superfood sausages and avocado and olive salad (p. 142)	leftover tandoori shrimp stir-fry and cucumber noodle salad with tomato (p. 148)	pressure cooker beef stew (p. 206)
Day 7	breakfast meatloaf (p. 60) and bacon-y sweet potato hash (p. 160)	leftover pressure cooker beef stew	pesto pasta with beef and olives (p. 122)

the 30 Day Guide to Paleo Cooking

Basic Ingredients

Nuts & Seeds
- ☐ Almonds, whole and slivered
- ☐ Macadamia nuts
- ☐ Pecans
- ☐ Pine nuts
- ☐ Walnuts

Produce
- ☐ Avocado
- ☐ Garlic
- ☐ Kalamata olives
- ☐ Lemons
- ☐ Limes

Oils & Fats
- ☐ Avocado oil
- ☐ Butter, grass-fed
- ☐ Coconut oil
- ☐ Duck fat or lard
- ☐ Ghee
- ☐ Macadamia nut oil
- ☐ Olive oil, extra-virgin
- ☐ Red palm oil
- ☐ Sesame oil
- ☐ Tallow
- ☐ Toasted sesame oil

Dried Spices
- ☐ Basil
- ☐ Black pepper
- ☐ Bay leaves
- ☐ Cayenne
- ☐ Chipotle powder
- ☐ Chinese 5-spice
- ☐ Cinnamon
- ☐ Coriander
- ☐ Cumin
- ☐ Curry
- ☐ Dill
- ☐ Fennel seeds
- ☐ Garam masala
- ☐ Garlic powder
- ☐ Ginger
- ☐ Marjoram
- ☐ Nutmeg
- ☐ Onion powder
- ☐ Old Bay seasoning
- ☐ Oregano
- ☐ Paprika
- ☐ Pumpkin pie spice
- ☐ Red pepper flakes
- ☐ Rosemary
- ☐ Sage (rubbed)
- ☐ Salt (sea & truffle)
- ☐ Sesame seeds
- ☐ Smoked paprika
- ☐ Thyme
- ☐ Turmeric
- ☐ White pepper

Vinegars
- ☐ Apple cider vinegar
- ☐ Balsamic vinegar
- ☐ White balsamic vinegar

Other
- ☐ Capers
- ☐ Chicken stock
- ☐ Coconut aminos
- ☐ Coconut milk
- ☐ Fish sauce
- ☐ Spicy brown mustard
- ☐ _____
- ☐ _____
- ☐ _____
- ☐ _____
- ☐ _____

the 30 Day Guide to Paleo Cooking

Meat

- ☐ Ahi tuna steak (day 2) - 1 (8 oz) steak
- ☐ Bacon - 2 lbs
- ☐ Beef bone broth (2 lbs beef marrow bones) – 6 cups, reserving one additional cup and freezing for a Week 2 recipe
- ☐ Beef liver - ½ lb
- ☐ Beef stew meat - 3 lbs
- ☐ Chicken bone broth (1 chicken back & neck) - 8 cups
- ☐ Chicken leg quarters - 2
- ☐ Chicken tenders - ½ lb
- ☐ Chops (lamb, goat or pork) - 4 chops
- ☐ Eggs - 2 dozen
- ☐ Flank steak - 1 ½ lbs
- ☐ Ground beef - 2 lbs
- ☐ Ground lamb (or beef) - 1 lb
- ☐ Ground pork - 4 lbs
- ☐ Ham - ½ cup cubed
- ☐ Shrimp, peeled, and de-veined (day 5) - 1 ½ lbs

Vegetables

- ☐ Asparagus – 2 ½ lbs
- ☐ Broccoli - 1 head
- ☐ Brussels sprouts - 2 cups
- ☐ Cabbage - 1 large, or 2 medium
- ☐ Carrots - 1 lb
- ☐ Celery - 1 head
- ☐ Cucumber- 3 medium
- ☐ Escarole - 1 head
- ☐ Green beans, french-style - 1 cup
- ☐ Green leaf lettuce - 2 heads
- ☐ Red bell peppers - 3
- ☐ Red potatoes - 4 small
- ☐ Shitake mushrooms - 2 cups
- ☐ Spaghetti squash - 2 large
- ☐ Spring mix salad greens - 9 cups
- ☐ Sweet potatoes - 3 large
- ☐ White mushrooms - 2 cups
- ☐ Yellow onions - 5 medium
- ☐ Yellow squash - 1 medium
- ☐ Zucchini - 2 medium

Fresh Herbs

- ☐ Basil - 1 large bunch
- ☐ Chives - 2 Tbsp
- ☐ Cilantro - ½ cup
- ☐ Oregano - 3 Tbsp
- ☐ Savory - 5 sprigs

Fruit

- ☐ Tomatoes - 1 Roma, 4 vine, 2 medium yellow, 2 cups grape tomatoes

Other

- ☐ Black sea salt to garnish (optional) - 2 Tbsp
- ☐ Diced tomatoes, no salt added - 1 can (15 oz)
- ☐ Pine nuts - 1/3 cup
- ☐ Tandoori - 1 Tbsp

Additional

- ☐ _____
- ☐ _____
- ☐ _____
- ☐ _____

the 30 Day Guide to Paleo Cooking

Enjoy
Meats

Vegetables

Fruits

Nuts

Seeds

Healthy Fats

Avoid
Grains

Legumes

Processed Dairy

Processed Foods

Alcohol

Soy + Seed Oils

Basic Shopping Guidelines

Always read the ingredients, and ditch any food item that has too many ingredients, strange ingredients, chemicals, sugars, food dyes, etc.

Eat pasture-raised meat. Pastured animal meat is the healthiest form of protein to consume because the animals were raised as they should be, and fed the diet they are supposed to eat. A healthy animal means a healthy you. The same goes for seafood: wild-caught is best, avoid farmed fish.

Shop in season for locally grown produce, try to find a good farmers market near you, join a CSA, or grow your own vegetables!

Don't skimp on fats. Always choose organic, unrefined oils, and only cook with heat-stable saturated fats. Avoid refined oils that are high in omega-6 fatty acids, also known as PUFAs.

Nuts and seeds are best consumed raw, and as a garnish—not as a staple item in your diet.

For more great recipes, menus, and meal planning tools, visit our website

www.PrimalPalate.com

Week 2 Meal Plan

	Breakfast	Lunch	Dinner
Day 8	leftover pesto pasta with beef and olives	baked chicken thigh wraps (p. 124) and leftover bacon-y sweet potato hash	lemon butter cod with tartar sauce (p. 94) and asparagus with gremolata (p. 158)
Day 9	leftover baked chicken thigh wraps	sesame beef stir-fry (p. 78)	paleo paella (p. 96)
Day 10	leftover sesame beef stir-fry	bacon wrapped mahi-mahi (p.88) and roasted cauliflower with caper relish (p. 170)	baked half-chicken (p. 134) and buttered squash ribbons (p.164)
Day 11	green eggs and ham with kale pesto (p. 68) and bacon, lettuce, and tomato salad (p. 144)	coffee break sliders (p. 104) and leftover bacon, lettuce, and tomato salad	fajita lettuce wraps with chipotle aioli (p. 106)
Day 12	leftover coffee break sliders	sesame tuna wraps (p.98)	shepherd's pie (p. 114) and roasted rosemary carrots with onion (p. 174)
Day 13	leftover shepherd's pie	meatballs with artichoke hearts (p. 118)	braised beef shanks (p. 184) and cabbage with onions and apples (p. 166)
Day 14	superfood sausages (p. 72) and leftover cabbage with onions and apples	harvest spiced drumsticks (p. 136) and asparagus with gremolata (p. 158)	pressure cooker pork roast (p. 188) and smoky roasted turnips with bacon (p. 176)

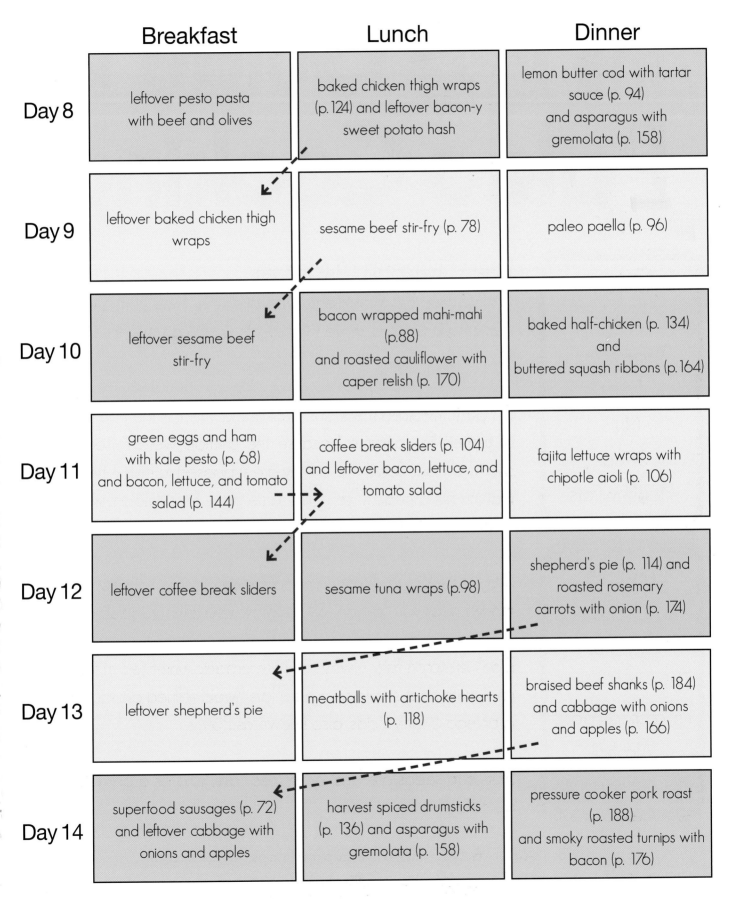

the 30 Day Guide to Paleo Cooking

Enjoy

Meats

Vegetables

Fruits

Nuts

Seeds

Healthy Fats

Avoid

Grains

Legumes

Processed Dairy

Processed Foods

Alcohol

Soy + Seed Oils

Basic Shopping Guidelines

Always read the ingredients, and ditch any food item that has too many ingredients, strange ingredients, chemicals, sugars, food dyes, etc.

Eat pasture-raised meat. Pastured animal meat is the healthiest form of protein to consume because the animals were raised as they should be, and fed the diet they are supposed to eat. A healthy animal means a healthy you. The same goes for seafood: wild-caught is best, avoid farmed fish.

Shop in season for locally grown produce, try to find a good farmers market near you, join a CSA, or grow your own vegetables!

Don't skimp on fats. Always choose organic, unrefined oils, and only cook with heat-stable saturated fats. Avoid refined oils that are high in omega-6 fatty acids, also known as PUFAs.

Nuts and seeds are best consumed raw, and as a garnish—not as a staple item in your diet.

For more great recipes, menus, and meal planning tools, visit our website

www.PrimalPalate.com

Meat

- ☐ Bacon - 1 lb
- ☐ Beef liver - ½ lb
- ☐ Beef shanks - 4 shanks
- ☐ Beef (steak) - 3 lbs
- ☐ Chicken - ½ of whole chicken
- ☐ Chicken breast, boneless and skinless - ½ lb
- ☐ Chicken drumsticks - 12
- ☐ Chicken thighs, bone in and skin on - 8
- ☐ Cod filet (day 8) - 1 lb
- ☐ Eggs - 4
- ☐ Flank steak - ½ lb
- ☐ Ground beef, pork or lamb - 2 lbs
- ☐ Ground pork - 3 lbs
- ☐ Ham - 6 slices
- ☐ Mahi-Mahi (day 10) - 1 ½ lbs
- ☐ Pork roast - 3-4 lbs
- ☐ Shrimp, peeled and deveined (day 9) - ½ lb
- ☐ Yellowtail tuna (day 12) - ¾ lb

Vegetables

- ☐ Artichoke hearts - 2 cups
- ☐ Asparagus - 4 lbs
- ☐ Carrots - 3 lbs
- ☐ Cauliflower - 4 heads
- ☐ Celery - 1 bunch
- ☐ Cucumber - ½ cup
- ☐ Green cabbage - 2 heads
- ☐ Green leaf lettuce - 1 head
- ☐ Green onion - 2 sprigs
- ☐ Iceberg lettuce - 2 large heads
- ☐ Kale - 2 cups
- ☐ Red bell peppers - 3
- ☐ Shiitake mushrooms - 2 cups
- ☐ Spaghetti squash - 1 medium
- ☐ Spring mix salad greens - 2 cups
- ☐ Turnips - 4 medium
- ☐ White mushrooms - 3 cups
- ☐ Yellow onions - 8 medium
- ☐ Yellow squash - 3 medium
- ☐ Zucchini - 3 medium

Fresh Herbs

- ☐ Basil - ½ cup
- ☐ Cilantro - 1 Tbsp
- ☐ Flat leaf parsley - 3 large bunches
- ☐ Fresh oregano - 2 Tbsp
- ☐ Thyme - 1 bunch

Fruit

- ☐ Green apples - 2
- ☐ Kumato (brown tomato) - 1
- ☐ Vine ripened tomatoes - 2

Other

- ☐ Coffee, finely ground - 1 Tbsp
- ☐ Pickles - 2 Tbsp
- ☐ Pine nuts - ⅓ cup
- ☐ Roasted nori sheets
- ☐ Saffron - 4 strands
- ☐ Water chestnuts - ½ cup

the 30 Day Guide to Paleo Cooking

Enjoy

Meats

Vegetables

Fruits

Nuts

Seeds

Healthy Fats

Avoid

Grains

Legumes

Processed Dairy

Processed Foods

Alcohol

Soy + Seed Oils

Basic Shopping Guidelines

Always read the ingredients, and ditch any food item that has too many ingredients, strange ingredients, chemicals, sugars, food dyes, etc.

Eat pasture-raised meat. Pastured animal meat is the healthiest form of protein to consume because the animals were raised as they should be, and fed the diet they are supposed to eat. A healthy animal means a healthy you. The same goes for seafood: wild-caught is best, avoid farmed fish.

Shop in season for locally grown produce, try to find a good farmers market near you, join a CSA, or grow your own vegetables!

Don't skimp on fats. Always choose organic, unrefined oils, and only cook with heat-stable saturated fats. Avoid refined oils that are high in omega-6 fatty acids, also known as PUFAs.

Nuts and seeds are best consumed raw, and as a garnish—not as a staple item in your diet.

For more great recipes, menus, and meal planning tools, visit our website

www.PrimalPalate.com

Week 3 Meal Plan

	Breakfast	Lunch	Dinner
Day 15	poached eggs with garlicky sprouts (p. 70)	leftover pressure cooker pork roast and leftover smoky roasted turnips with bacon	garlic ginger chicken (p. 132) and roasted cauliflower with caper relish (p. 170)
Day 16	egg custards (p. 66)	tomato braised short ribs (p. 192) and mashed cauliflower, double batch (p. 210)	italian wedding soup (p. 204)
Day 17	leftover tomato braised short ribs	leftover italian wedding soup	teriyaki baby back ribs (p. 84) and leftover mashed cauliflower
Day 18	leftover italian wedding soup	leftover teriyaki baby back ribs and leftover mashed cauliflower	beef brisket (p. 182) and broccoli and leek soup (p. 198)
Day 19	broccoli casserole (p. 62)	leftover beef brisket and leftover broccoli and leek soup	bison stew (p. 194)
Day 20	leftover broccoli casserole	leftover bison stew	pasta with meatballs (p. 120)
Day 21	leftover pasta with meatballs	sesame tuna wraps (p. 98)	crispy truffle chicken with herbs (p. 128) and mashed cauliflower (p. 210) and roasted rosemary carrots with onion (p. 174)

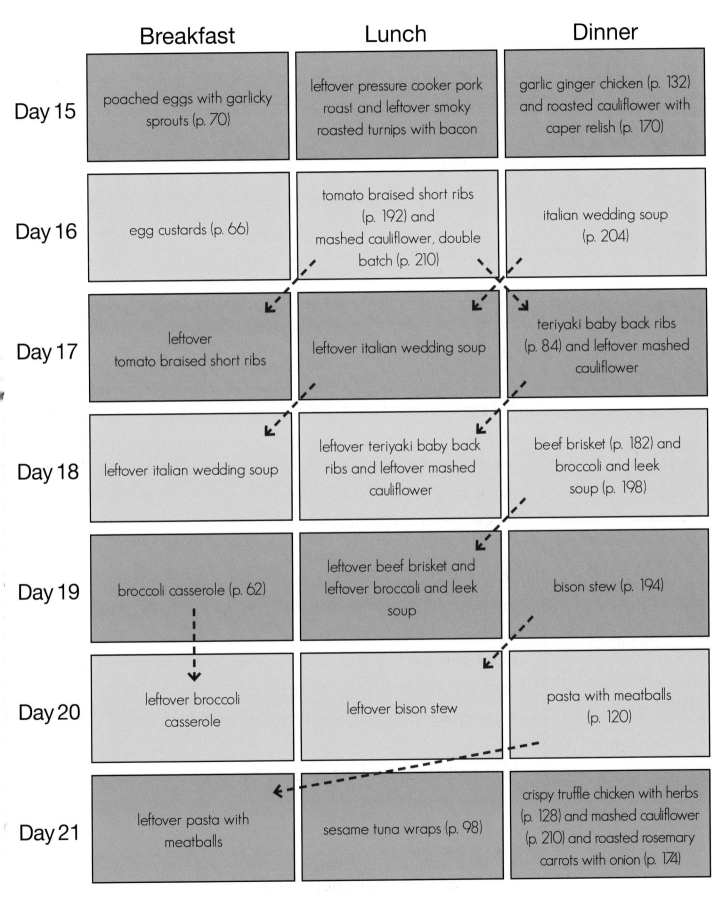

the 30 Day Guide to Paleo Cooking

Enjoy

Meats

Vegetables

Fruits

Nuts

Seeds

Healthy Fats

Avoid

Grains

Legumes

Processed Dairy

Processed Foods

Alcohol

Soy + Seed Oils

Basic Shopping Guidelines

Always read the ingredients, and ditch any food item that has too many ingredients, strange ingredients, chemicals, sugars, food dyes, etc.

Eat pasture-raised meat. Pastured animal meat is the healthiest form of protein to consume because the animals were raised as they should be, and fed the diet they are supposed to eat. A healthy animal means a healthy you. The same goes for seafood: wild-caught is best, avoid farmed fish.

Shop in season for locally grown produce, try to find a good farmers market near you, join a CSA, or grow your own vegetables!

Don't skimp on fats. Always choose organic, unrefined oils, and only cook with heat-stable saturated fats. Avoid refined oils that are high in omega-6 fatty acids, also known as <u>PUFAs.</u>

Nuts and seeds are best consumed raw, and as a garnish—not as a staple item in your diet.

For more great recipes, menus, and meal planning tools, visit our website

www.PrimalPalate.com

the 30 Day Guide to Paleo Cooking

Meat

- ☐ Bacon - ½ lb
- ☐ Beef bone broth (2 lbs beef marrow bones) - 8 cups, reserving 2 cups to freeze for a Week 4 recipe
- ☐ Beef brisket - 2 lbs
- ☐ Beef short ribs - 5 lbs
- ☐ Bison steak medallions (stew meat) - 2 lbs
- ☐ Chicken thighs - 8
- ☐ Chicken stock (2 chicken backs & necks – 2 batches) - 13 cups
- ☐ Chicken, whole - 6 lbs
- ☐ Eggs - 15
- ☐ Ground pork - 5 lbs
- ☐ Pork baby back ribs - 3 lbs
- ☐ _____
- ☐ _____
- ☐ _____
- ☐ _____
- ☐ _____

Vegetables

- ☐ Broccoli - 4 heads
- ☐ Brussels sprouts - 2 cups
- ☐ Carrots - 2 lbs
- ☐ Cauliflower - 5 heads
- ☐ Celery - 1 bunch
- ☐ Escarole - 1 head
- ☐ Green onion (garnish) - ¼ cup
- ☐ Leek - 1 stalk
- ☐ Spaghetti squash - 1 medium
- ☐ White mushrooms - 5 cups
- ☐ Yellow onions - 5 medium
- ☐ _____
- ☐ _____
- ☐ _____
- ☐ _____

Fresh Herbs

- ☐ Chives - 2 Tbsp
- ☐ Fresh ginger root - 1 Tbsp
- ☐ Thyme - 3 sprigs
- ☐ Rosemary - 3 sprigs

Other

- ☐ Black olives - ¼ cup
- ☐ Strained tomatoes - 2 cups
- ☐ Tomato paste - 1 small can (6 oz)
- ☐ Tomato sauce (Muir Glen, no salt added) - 3 cans, 15 oz each

Additional

- ☐ _____
- ☐ _____
- ☐ _____
- ☐ _____
- ☐ _____
- ☐ _____
- ☐ _____
- ☐ _____

the 30 Day Guide to Paleo Cooking

Enjoy

Meats

Vegetables

Fruits

Nuts

Seeds

Healthy Fats

Avoid

Grains

Legumes

Processed Dairy

Processed Foods

Alcohol

Soy + Seed Oils

Basic Shopping Guidelines

Always read the ingredients, and ditch any food item that has too many ingredients, strange ingredients, chemicals, sugars, food dyes, etc.

Eat pasture-raised meat. Pastured animal meat is the healthiest form of protein to consume because the animals were raised as they should be, and fed the diet they are supposed to eat. A healthy animal means a healthy you. The same goes for seafood: wild-caught is best, avoid farmed fish.

Shop in season for locally grown produce, try to find a good farmers market near you, join a CSA, or grow your own vegetables!

Don't skimp on fats. Always choose organic, unrefined oils, and only cook with heat-stable saturated fats. Avoid refined oils that are high in omega-6 fatty acids, also known as PUFAs.

Nuts and seeds are best consumed raw, and as a garnish—not as a staple item in your diet.

For more great recipes, menus, and meal planning tools, visit our website

www.PrimalPalate.com

Week 4 Meal Plan

	Breakfast	Lunch	Dinner
Day 22	green eggs and ham with kale pesto (p. 68) and almond flour pancakes (p. 56)	leftover crispy truffle chicken with herbs and leftover mashed cauliflower and leftover roasted rosemary carrots with onion	paleo paella (p. 96)
Day 23	lamb chops two ways (p. 76)	pesto pasta with beef and olives (p. 122)	coffee-marinated flat iron steaks (p. 64) and bacon, lettuce, and tomato salad (p. 144)
Day 24	leftover coffee-marinated flat iron steaks and leftover bacon, lettuce and tomato salad	leftover pesto pasta with beef and olives	rump roast under pressure (p. 190) and cream of mushroom soup (p. 202)
Day 25	leftover rump roast under pressure and leftover cream of mushroom soup	cobb salad (p. 146)	garlic and dill sockeye salmon (p. 92) and mashed cauliflower (p. 210)
Day 26	leftover garlic and dill sockeye salmon and leftover mashed cauliflower	chicken soup with bone broth (p. 200)	skillet chicken leg quarters (p. 140)
Day 27	leftover chicken soup with bone broth	cherry balsamic pasta (p. 116)	grilled ahi tuna nicoise (p. 150)
Day 28	egg custards (p. 66)	leftover cherry balsamic pasta	meatloaf (p. 112) and smoky roasted turnips with bacon (p. 176)
Day 29	leftover meatloaf and leftover smoky roasted turnips with bacon	sesame-ginger flank steak salad (p. 154)	duck a l'orange (p. 130) and cucumber noodle salad with tomato (p. 148)
Day 30	leftover sesame-ginger flank steak salad	leftover duck a l'orange	pad thai with chicken (p. 138)

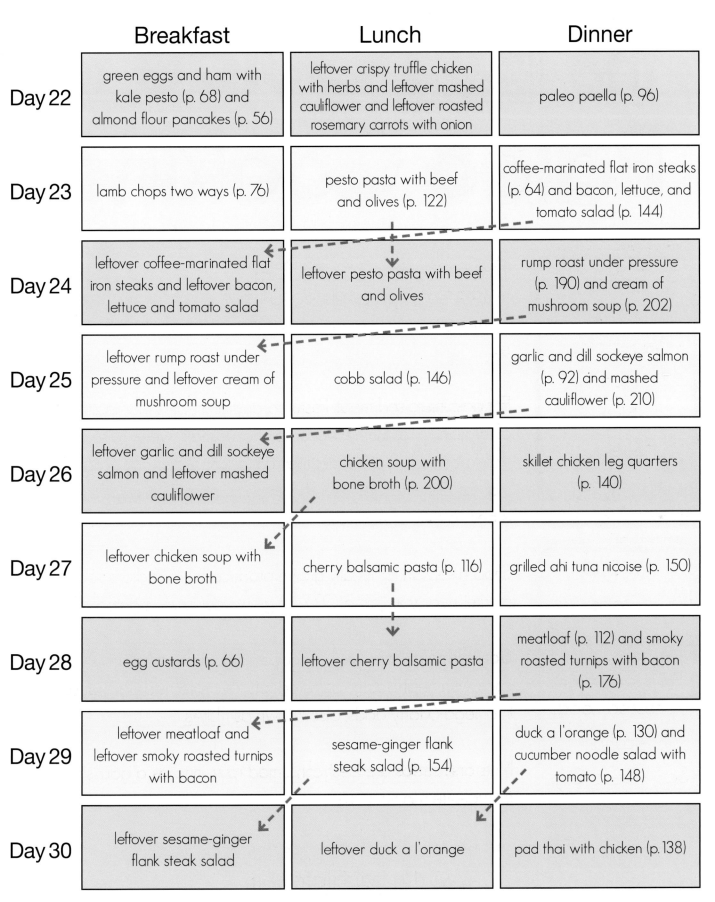

the 30 Day Guide to Paleo Cooking

Enjoy

Meats

Vegetables

Fruits

Nuts

Seeds

Healthy Fats

Avoid

Grains

Legumes

Processed Dairy

Processed Foods

Alcohol

Soy + Seed Oils

Basic Shopping Guidelines

Always read the ingredients, and ditch any food item that has too many ingredients, strange ingredients, chemicals, sugars, food dyes, etc.

Eat pasture-raised meat. Pastured animal meat is the healthiest form of protein to consume because the animals were raised as they should be, and fed the diet they are supposed to eat. A healthy animal means a healthy you. The same goes for seafood: wild-caught is best, avoid farmed fish.

Shop in season for locally grown produce, try to find a good farmers market near you, join a CSA, or grow your own vegetables!

Don't skimp on fats. Always choose organic, unrefined oils, and only cook with heat-stable saturated fats. Avoid refined oils that are high in omega-6 fatty acids, also known as PUFAs.

Nuts and seeds are best consumed raw, and as a garnish—not as a staple item in your diet.

For more great recipes, menus, and meal planning tools, visit our website

www.PrimalPalate.com

the 30 Day Guide to Paleo Cooking

Meat

- ☐ Ahi tuna steak (day 27) - ¾ lb
- ☐ Bacon - 1 lb (save bacon fat for other recipes)
- ☐ Beef bone broth (should be frozen from Week 3) - 2 cups
- ☐ Beef liver - ½ lb
- ☐ Beef rump roast - 3 ½ lbs
- ☐ Chicken bone broth (2 chicken backs and necks) - 4 quarts
- ☐ Chicken breast, boneless skinless - 1 ½ lbs
- ☐ Chicken leg quarters - 2
- ☐ Chicken tenders - ½ lb
- ☐ Chicken thighs, boneless and skinless - 16
- ☐ Duck, whole with skin - 5 lbs
- ☐ Eggs - 18
- ☐ Flank steak - 1 ½ lbs
- ☐ Flat iron steaks - 4
- ☐ Ground beef or lamb - 2 ½ lbs
- ☐ Ground beef - 3 lbs
- ☐ Ham - 6 slices + 1 cup cubed
- ☐ Lamb chops - 6
- ☐ Shrimp (day 22) - ½ lb
- ☐ Sockeye salmon (day 25) - ¾ lb

Vegetables

- ☐ Asparagus - 1 ½ lbs
- ☐ Carrots - 2 lbs
- ☐ Cauliflower - 2 head
- ☐ Celery - 2 heads
- ☐ Cucumbers - 3
- ☐ Green leaf lettuce - 2 heads
- ☐ Iceberg lettuce - ½ cup
- ☐ Kale - 2 cups
- ☐ Red bell peppers - 2
- ☐ Shallots - 2
- ☐ Spaghetti squash - 3 medium
- ☐ Spring mix salad greens - 6 cups
- ☐ Turnips - 4
- ☐ White mushrooms - 3 cups
- ☐ Yellow onions - 8 medium
- ☐ Yellow squash - 4 medium

Fruit

- ☐ Grape tomatoes - 2 cups
- ☐ Kumato (brown tomato) - 1
- ☐ Lemons (for juice) - 2
- ☐ Orange - 1
- ☐ Roma tomato - 1
- ☐ Vine ripe tomato - 1

Fresh Herbs

- ☐ Basil - 1 large bunch (at least 3 packed cups)
- ☐ Chives - 2 Tbsp
- ☐ Cilantro - 1 Tbsp
- ☐ Flat leaf parsley - 1 large bunch
- ☐ Oregano - 1 small bunch
- ☐ Thyme - 3 sprigs

Other

- ☐ Almond butter - ¼ cup
- ☐ Bacon fat - 2 Tbsp
- ☐ Blanched almond flour - 1 ¾ cups
- ☐ Cherry balsamic vinegar - ⅓ cup
- ☐ Coffee, ground - 1 Tbsp
- ☐ Diced tomatoes, no salt added - 1 can (15 oz)
- ☐ Macadamia nuts - ⅓ cup
- ☐ Pine nuts - ⅔ cup
- ☐ Roasted nori sheets
- ☐ Saffron - 4 strands
- ☐ Tomato paste - 1 small can (6 oz)
- ☐ Vanilla
- ☐ Grass-fed butter

the **30 Day** Guide to Paleo Cooking

Enjoy

Meats

Vegetables

Fruits

Nuts

Seeds

Healthy Fats

Avoid

Grains

Legumes

Processed Dairy

Processed Foods

Alcohol

Soy + Seed Oils

Basic Shopping Guidelines

Always read the ingredients, and ditch any food item that has too many ingredients, strange ingredients, chemicals, sugars, food dyes, etc.

Eat pasture-raised meat. Pastured animal meat is the healthiest form of protein to consume because the animals were raised as they should be, and fed the diet they are supposed to eat. A healthy animal means a healthy you. The same goes for seafood: wild-caught is best, avoid farmed fish.

Shop in season for locally grown produce, try to find a good farmers market near you, join a CSA, or grow your own vegetables!

Don't skimp on fats. Always choose organic, unrefined oils, and only cook with heat-stable saturated fats. Avoid refined oils that are high in omega-6 fatty acids, also known as <u>PUFAs</u>.

Nuts and seeds are best consumed raw, and as a garnish—not as a staple item in your diet.

For more great recipes, menus, and meal planning tools, visit our website

www.PrimalPalate.com